J.K. LASSER PRO™

KEEPING CLIENTS FOR LIFE

The *J.K. Lasser Pro* Series

The *Wiley Financial Advisor* Series

J.K. LASSER PRO™

KEEPING CLIENTS
FOR LIFE

Karen Caplan Altfest

John Wiley & Sons, Inc.
New York • Chichester • Weinheim • Brisbane • Singapore • Toronto

Published by John Wiley & Sons, Inc.
Published simultaneously in Canada.

Library of Congress Cataloging-in-Publication Data:

ISBN 0-471-40881-6

Printed in the United States of America.

10   9   8   7   6   5   4   3   2   1

To Lew Altfest and the dedicated financial planning, investment, and administrative team at L.J. Altfest & Co., Inc.

Contents

Preface

Keeping Clients for Life is written expressly to help financial service professionals build up their practices by understanding clients and responding to their needs. This book will help financial professionals relate to their clients in a meaningful way, recognize what drives clients' thoughts and actions, understand their deep-rooted psychological needs, and develop the people skills necessary to win prospects and keep clients for life.

Through examples, stories, conversations, action steps, and other tools that have been tested, readers learn that the key to building a successful practice is knowing that clients value a good, honest relationship as much as they do financial expertise from an advisor. You can learn how to be that trusted advisor for your clients.

Keeping Clients for Life is organized to follow the progression of the client-planner relationship from the first phone call, through the initial meeting, to the presentation of the plan. It takes readers through the steps needed to establish goals, determine lifestyle choices, deal with family issues, present the plan, follow up, and maintain an ongoing connection that satisfies you and your clients. Readers learn how much of themselves to give to clients, how to converse comfortably, how to form relationships with other professionals, and how to become a media resource. The author stresses the nature and importance of top-notch service and methods of evaluating your performance as a service provider.

The author, Karen Caplan Altfest, Ph.D., CFP, is vice president of L.J. Altfest & Co., Inc., fee-only financial planners and investment managers. She is nationally known for her professional expertise, communication skills, and work with female clients and their families. She was coordinator of the CFP program at Pace University and currently directs the investment program in continuing education at the New School in New York City.

Dr. Altfest has written many articles for professional journals and consumer magazines on practice management and financial planning topics and frequently serves as a financial expert for television and print media. She has recently been quoted in *Working Woman*, the *New York Times*, the *Wall Street Journal*, *Investment News*, *New York Daily News*, *Newsday*, *Los Angeles Times*, *Medical Economics*, *Spirit*, *Family Money*, *Financial Planning*, *Bottom Line* and *Mutual Funds* magazine. She has lectured to the AAII, AARP, AICPA, NAPFA, FPA, and many other organizations. She has appeared on NBC, CNBC, CNN, Fox Television, CBS, and New York 1. Dr. Altfest is included in *Who's Who in America*, *Who's Who in Finance*, and *Who's Who of American Women*. She serves as president of the Northeast/MidAtlantic Region of the National Association of Personal Financial Advisors and as a director for public relations of the New York chapter of the Financial Planning Association.

Dr. Altfest has changed the names and some details of client situations presented in this book to protect the anonymity of her clients. Dr. Altfest, her husband Lew, and their two grown children live in New York City and Connecticut.

Acknowledgments

Thanks are due to Lew Altfest who commented on the manuscript and to Frances Minters who offered many meaningful suggestions. Thanks, too, to my agent, Andrea Pedolsky, for encouraging and assisting me at the proposal stage, and to my editor, Debra Englander, for overseeing the project.

Introduction

Financial Well-Being

True financial planning involves more than crunching numbers. It encompasses the many issues beyond dollars and cents that concern your clients and their families. Your clients are multidimensional beings with layers of emotional, psychological, personal, and financial needs that are often difficult to separate. The successful financial planner who forms long-lasting relationships with clients learns about clients' backgrounds, hopes, wishes, families, and personal stories *before* prescribing financial solutions to their problems.

Think about your clients' financial well-being in much the same way physicians consider their patients' physical well-being. Do not let one obvious symptom of financial malaise distract you from doing due diligence for the entire person or family. While a quick fix often appeals to clients and can be simple for planners in much the same way that a sugar pill can dull a pain, it does not lead to true problem solving nor long-term solutions. By examining and then treating the total person and financial goals, lifestyle considerations, family issues, and personal dreams, you may have a client for life.

The Financial Planning Wheel

I always picture my clients standing in the middle of a circle. Figure I.1 shows the financial planning wheel that contains clients and revolves around them. Clients are surrounded by the six areas of financial planning: cash management, risk management, tax, investment, retirement, and estate planning. They have choices and decisions, opportunities, and responsibilities in each of these areas, and what they do in any one area will certainly resonate in the others.

The Circle of Life

I also picture a second wider circle outside the first. This is the circle of life that affects the client: immediate family, extended family, friends and colleagues, job, hobbies, commitments, location, emotional aspects, psychological aspects, health, and age (see Figure I.2). Each area defines a part of the client's life. All these and many other variables impact the client in obvious and subtle ways, which then reverberate in the financial area. Neither circle is independent of the other. Good planners deal with the six financial areas contained in the financial planning wheel; great planners also deal with the circle of life. That is

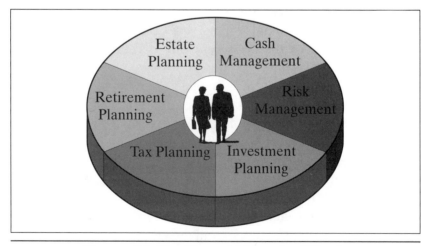

FIGURE I.1 The Financial Planning Wheel.

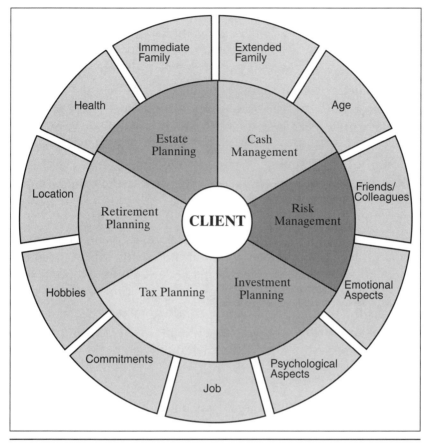

FIGURE I.2 The Circle of Life.

why it is so important to question, prod, and get to know many personal and private things about your clients from the first meeting on.

Psychological Underpinnings

Yes, good financial planning does have a psychological component. The relationship between the advisor and client (or client's family) is often similar to one between a therapist and a patient. Good listening skills, empathy, and patience are key ingredients; learning to question and encourage people to reveal their inner feelings, hopes, beliefs, motivations, and even their childhood experiences can be paramount to accomplishing good work. You cannot fake interest in these areas, but you can learn to hone your skills.

As a planner, you may be called on to engage family members and mediate between them. Your clients who are members of different generations may have opposing issues, while spouses you meet may have unresolved battles in many areas of their lives. Questions that seem to deal with money may have strong undercurrents of sibling rivalry or adult children's drives for independence. Your professional ability to present calm alternatives to a family in a state of flux can be important to the resolution of old sores.

The members of one family I met recently were concerned about finding good advice for their widowed, elderly mother. One brother and two sisters, they had been to three planners but had not agreed to hire anyone. The first planner had been proposed by the brother, a take-charge individual who dismissed his sisters as unknowledgeable and self-centered. They opposed his choice. The second planner was a friend of one of the sisters, but did not gain the respect of the other siblings. The third planner had been recommended by the youngest sister's husband, but was dismissed as not being serious enough. Finally, the middle sister asked her colleagues for a recommendation, which is how they came to my firm. The family was looking for someone with no prior connections to any sibling (to eliminate jealousy), someone with strong professional credentials (to strengthen objective criteria), and a planner who could empathize with the personal relations involved in their particular scenario.

I have been hired by many adult children to help their elderly parents. Whether it is an only child saddled with the total responsibility for a parent's well-being, or a group of four siblings, the situations are often tense. When there is more than one adult child, it is unusual for them to be of one mind. They may agree that their parent's financial health is paramount, but disagree about what constitutes that desired state. One sibling might think selling the family home is best for the parent; another might argue that the parent should stay in the family home forever. Childhood feelings about the home, and feelings like "Mom always listened to you more than to me," have to be resolved before the whole picture can be seen.

As an advisor, you must use skills and wisdom to draw people out, comfort them, and lead them toward resolution. The process requires talking, illustrating, listening, brainstorming, and sharing stories and ideas.

As in psychotherapy, the emotional needs of the client are often transferred to the advisor. Some clients expect their advisors to reassure them, take care of them, and frequently pay undue attention to their needs. I have a client who has been fired by lawyers, accountants, and does not have very good relationships with her children. She feels constantly rejected, yet insists on a level of service that almost ensures her advisors will fail to meet her demands, and therefore not live up to her expectations. This woman can fax me as many as 8 to 10 requests a day on issues ranging from taxation to investments to employment to housing. Some of her concerns go back as many as 16 or 17 years, predating my business relationship with her. Her constant demands and inquiries are unrealistic, yet if they are not immediately addressed she becomes surly and annoyed. So far, I have managed to handle her demands; I am still hanging in there, because I know she needs financial help and hand-holding with a velvet glove.

Other clients are satisfied by a more normal level of hand-holding. They just require frequent reassurance that the market is not going to decline to zero (or, as one client said, dissolve in a puff of smoke), that their retirement is secure, and that they are working well toward their goals. The key to giving them comfort is to treat each conversation as important, handle each request as something new and relevant, and take time to Listen (with a capital *L*).

Keeping Clients for Life will help you relate more effectively to your clients, recognize the underlying message in their conversations, understand that their needs are more than financial, and develop your people skills. As an outgrowth, sensitivity to your clients' emotional and psychological needs will make you a more accessible and sought after financial planner. Your business success is ultimately linked to your clients' satisfaction.

First Meeting: On the Telephone

What Do Prospective Clients Really Want?

Ostensibly, prospective clients call a financial planner to determine whether the firm provides the services they need and what the costs of working together would be. Some of this information they can likely get from an ad in the telephone directory or from a brochure. The client's unstated questions—what motivates the initial phone call—are really, can we get along? Will you listen to me and hear what I want? Can you give me what I need? Will this be a comfortable relationship? This first brief conversation is your opportunity to address these issues by engaging prospects in a focused and meaningful dialogue.

A prospect may have been referred by a friend, or have seen your name in a newspaper article or even in the yellow pages of the telephone directory. A small number of people are very trusting and seem eager to begin a relationship. Most callers are on an exploratory mission, calling several advisors with no particular pattern and no preconceived outcome.

When prospects call a professional office for information, they may be curt, they may be very guarded, and they would like to know if you will be sympathetic to their situations, but often find they are given only a machine on which to leave a name and address. This reinforces their fear that they will be just a name and number at your firm. Probably they hoped for an initial contact with a professional and a reason to take the step toward forming a relationship. Think about whether an answering machine conveys the greeting you wish first-time callers to experience. If yes, make sure you return all calls promptly; if no, hire an assistant or an answering service to provide human contact for your prospects.

At my office, I am determined to find a link, something of interest that we can talk about even before we meet. I talk to most prospects because I enjoy getting to know new people, unless my assistant determines that the caller is inappropriate for our firm. Recently, a woman called from several hundred miles away because her husband asked her to get my brochure. Within five minutes, I discovered that she had two children in college, she lives where my daughter went to school, and I live where her daughter goes to school. Guess what we talked about? As she put it, "Country bumpkins go to the big city, while kids who grow up in the city go to the country." Before we hung up, we made an appointment, one that I am really looking forward to. Engaging callers in a conversation about their personal situations gives you an opportunity to hear their concerns, labels you as someone who is interested in them, and can convince them that it is worthwhile to visit your office.

Getting to Know Prospective Clients in a Phone Call

If you enjoy talking to people, and believe that everyone has an interesting story to tell, you are ahead of the game. The more information you gather, the easier it will be to get a prospect to visit your office, and the more likely you are to win them as a client. You will also have the opportunity to screen appropriate clients based on their information and refer others to colleagues.

For wary callers who initiate contact but are reluctant to reveal themselves, try to find a topic that encourages them to open up. The process is somewhat analogous to sitting next to strangers on an airplane and hearing their whole life story before the plane arrives at its destination. For example, on a flight returning from a meeting, my seatmate, a young woman, told me about her attempts to get pregnant (none of which was successful) and then described her close relationships with her young nieces and nephews!

Drawing out a caller is as easy as 1-2-3. Ask them:

- What kind of work they do, or if they are retired. Most people will at least give you the basics of their employment situation.

- Whether they are married and if they have children. People really enjoy talking about their families.

- Where their money is now. People can't resist telling you if they have done something they are proud of, if they feel inadequate about managing their funds, or if they have an advisor who they do or do not care for. They might even point out problems they have had, or opportunities they feel they have missed.

Notice these are all questions, things to *ask* the caller, not information to *give* them. If you lead by asking questions, you will elicit useful information and engage the caller in discussing the topic they know best—their own unique circumstances. The alternative, talking about yourself or your firm too soon, can be off-putting. You might answer the caller's surface questions but risk ending the conversation before you have a chance to make a connection with the caller, which should be a main goal of your conversation. You want to break down the natural barriers that occur between strangers, introduce the human element (otherwise you could have a machine taking your phone messages), and lay the groundwork to move to the next level of personal interaction with your potential new client.

Of course, each question and answer can and should lead to many others. As long as the caller is telling you things about herself, you should be listening, making notes (it will help you focus and provide a structure for your first face-to-face meeting), and leading her to reveal more and more about her personal and financial situation. Since you cannot see the caller, and so cannot take advantage of visual body language cues, you need to be extra sensitive to verbal nuance. Note how casual, emotional, or guarded the caller seems. Then you can respond to those signals appropriately.

Frequently, prospects have not yet thought out the specific services they want, and quite likely have not thoroughly considered their goals in meeting with a financial professional. As a result, when you ask prospective clients what financial services interest them, they are uncertain and reply, "What do you mean?" as if you somehow should sense what they need. If you then suggest some services that you offer, such as planning for retirement or reviewing investments, they should relax and begin to clarify what they want. Another approach to opening up is to ask callers what financial concerns they have. This usually encourages callers to explain some of the issues that are troubling them— and you can begin to put their concerns into a professional framework.

Do not talk generalities about the stock market or speak in financialese. Jargon is a real turnoff and actually makes people feel left out rather than included in what you have to say. By listening to the caller and engaging in preliminary conversation, you are letting that person know you are interested in your client's overall well-being. At the same time, you are setting the foundation for a comfortable situation when you and the caller actually get together. When this caller meets you, he will not feel that he is embarking on a new relationship, but that he is picking up from where the phone call left off. And you can use the information you gather over the phone to propel your face-to-face meeting to the next level. This includes developing a natural telephone conversational style, just as you would if you were seated across from the prospect, or from someone you met at a social gathering. Your questions should not be challenging or threatening. Your specific questions targeted to the caller's situations should show how interested you are.

A sample telephone conversation with prodding from the planner might be:

Planner: Are you currently working?

Caller: Yes, I am.

Planner: (*Prodding*) What kind of work do you do?

Caller: I am an attorney.

Planner: Oh, do you have your own practice?

Caller:	I used to, but I recently joined ABC bank in its trust department.
Planner:	(*Responding to the caller's cues*) Yes, I know them. I have some clients who work there. (*Prodding*) Why did you join the bank?
Caller:	I was tired of running my own law office. It became too much work. The bank made me an offer, and I decided to take it.
Planner:	How long have you been there?
Caller:	I have worked at the bank two years, and I plan to stay until my 60th birthday, in four more years.

Now, after just a few minutes, the planner knows what the prospect does, how long he has been doing it, how old he is, and when he plans to retire. Even better, the door to an exchange of information has been opened, the caller's barriers have been let down, and the planner can proceed to gather more personal details.

Interviewing techniques should be practiced and honed so that it does not seem as if you are grilling prospects, a sure way to discourage anyone from coming to meet you. It is also effective to give a little information back to the caller when appropriate. It shows you have been listening, that you care, and that you understand where he is coming from. You might say, "Many of our clients are attorneys," or for a different type of connection, "It is difficult for lawyers to keep up their hectic pace after age 60."

Moving on to the caller's family, an appropriate follow-up question could be, what sort of work does your wife do? To ask about the caller's forthcoming retirement, probe with the questions, where will you go when you retire? Will you stay in your current home?

One of my favorite questions, but only after I have established some rapport and covered the basics, is "What made you think of calling?" This is more open-ended than the other questions, and causes the caller to think deeply about motivation, generating very useful information. While the other answers are about family and job that most people would freely give to anyone, this question leads to highly personal thinking.

Now, look at all the information you have. You know what the caller does, where he does it, how long he has been there, what he did prior, and when he expects to retire. You may even have some information about his spouse. He knows that you are attentive to his situation, which leads him to start thinking about what he hopes to accomplish in this new relationship. Most important, you have begun to develop a relationship of concern and interest.

Allowing Callers to Open Up

Although your first assumption should be that people want to talk about themselves, you still have to build a bridge over the telephone that allows them to do so. If you talk about yourself or the economy, and you are one of three financial advisors they contact that day, they may well remember nothing you say by the end of the call. If, however, you allow the caller to feel secure enough by your phone presence that she can open up to you, she will have memories of an encouraging, enthusiastic, sympathetic being on the other end of the line. In other words, people like people who care about them.

What should always be foremost in your thoughts is wanting to provide an environment that encourages the communication of privileged information, and treating what you hear as an exchange between trusted confidants. Do not pass judgment on anything you hear (how many times have I heard "I got my money in an unconventional way"?). You certainly may choose not to meet prospects with an unusual history, or people with other problems (e.g., considerable debt, a low savings rate, bankruptcy filings, unrealistic expectations, unusual family situations, poor records, lost money on investments, etc.) even though other planners may be attracted to just those circumstances. If you find you truly cannot be sympathetic to a caller's situation, consider referring him to another professional or even an organization that deals with his situation.

I have referred people to Debtor's Anonymous, Consumer Credit Counseling Service, and other organizations, and the callers always seem pleased to learn such organizations exist. I have given them the number to call for a list of planners in their area, and I have made referrals to newer planners in my community. Another planner I know actually sends troubled callers for psychological counseling, and they have called back to thank him. Not every caller is a good match for your practice, and that is okay. Do not judge your success on the amount of prospects you convert to clients, but on the quality of the fit for your firm.

Setting Up the Interview

You should speak to prospects on the phone only when you have time for a substantial interview, not when you are about to dash off to a meeting or assume some other imminent task. While you are on the phone, you want to think only of the caller and what she is telling you, not about all the things you have to do later in the day. Use your keyboard if that helps you track the conversation, but beware—typing information into your database can turn your attention away from the caller, which could suggest a lack of interest and make her wonder if you are more concerned with recording name, age, salary, and assets than you are in getting to know the person behind the call. Better to jot down your notes with pen and paper and enter them into your database after the call.

Provide a nurturing, safe environment so that people are willing to tell you things about themselves they are not used to sharing. Think of your initial task as over-the-phone hand-holding. If you are not the kind of person who finds it easy to be supportive to others, take classes, practice, and hone those skills. Remember the times you went to a new doctor's office as a first-time patient and were asked for background information. What made it pleasant or unpleasant? I once left a crowded doctor's office after I had been kept waiting for two hours. That evening, the doctor whom I had not yet met called to apologize. I rescheduled and saw the doctor a few times, but my initial impression of a too-crowded, disorganized, impersonal office was proved correct. I was never happy there, had delays and other problems each time I visited, and after two years left him for another doctor.

Hopefully, if you are unable to adapt your style to the needs, concerns, and well-being of callers, someone in your office is better suited to answer your phones and return prospect inquiries.

Remember, the biggest concern of new callers is that you care about them and their problems. If you can convey that you honestly care, you will be a winner in the new prospect lottery in your town.

When you return a prospective client's call, ask if this is a good time to talk. If the person feels uncomfortable because someone in her office is nearby, or he is expecting a repairman to ring the doorbell at home, he or she will not be forthcoming, and you will have lost the chance to make a connection. Try to avoid telephone tag. It can be unnerving to a prospective client to speak repeatedly to your voice mail and hear from you only on a machine. Better to arrange a telephone appointment and call back at a mutually convenient time than to lose the opportunity to get to know the person on the other end of the line. And you cannot address their concerns, or show understanding of their problems, if you have not had a chance to hear them.

Should You Send Out a Questionnaire Before Seeing the Client?

Some planners are so guarded about their time they will not see anyone who has not filled out a questionnaire that details personal and financial circumstances. This no doubt helps them make a good match with a new prospect, and may save them time during their busy schedules. However, many prospective clients are offended by getting the questionnaire before they have had a chance to meet with and assess the planner, and refuse to answer personal questions about their income and assets on a piece of paper. I have been told this many times over the years by clients who have refused to go to planners who will not see them without a preliminary questionnaire and have come to my firm instead.

Your job is to weigh the pluses of time saved by a questionnaire against the minuses of alienating potentially good clients by jumping the gun. If you do send out a preliminary questionnaire, keep it brief and do not expect specific asset or income figures. Many people will not divulge those numbers except in a safe and private setting. If a preliminary questionnaire is not for you, try to think of other time savers, such as briefer phone interviews, returning calls only at the end of the day, preliminary screening by an associate in your office, or sending a package of information about your company to prospects so that they come in to meet you with realistic expectations.

Who Is Likely to Come Aboard; Who Is Unlikely to but May Crop Up Like a Weed Every Other Season

I have people who call me every fall, as regular as the leaves turn red and yellow. They tell me they wanted to become a client in the past, but some part of their lives delayed them. They inevitably say that this time they are ready to proceed, but a little voice tells me they probably never will. A few times a year, I hear from people who say they spoke to me (or heard me speak publicly) a couple of years ago. When I find their files, our conversation was often four or five or six years earlier. Repeat callers usually go all the way down the road, including the telephone conversation, setting up an appointment, coming in for an interview, exchanging documents, but they never sign the agreement and I never do their work. They may be afraid to commit to a professional relationship or may be long-standing delayers. You have to decide how far you want to proceed with this kind of prospect.

Prospects You Do Not Want to Become Clients

Parents may be stuck with an undesirable trait in their child, spouses may have to put up with some irrational behavior, but you do not have to accept clients who will make your life more difficult and demand too much of your time. Just as your clients can select you, you can select them. Listen closely to your prospects' remarks about relationships with other advisors. They may be telling you something you need to consider carefully. If a prospect has fired her attorney, accountant, and stockbroker, you should think about why you are getting involved. You will probably be the next to go. And, like a divorce, the process of parting ways can bring much anguish. If the prospect has recently sued two other advisors, or not paid his fees, stay away.

Some years ago, a very agitated man walked into my office. He told me his last advisor fired him, and he did not know why. He

Four Clunkers and the Psychology Driving Them

Clunker Number One—Never Ties the Knot. Recently, I received a phone call from a man who said he had called my firm a few years ago for information but had never followed up. Now he said he wanted to take care of his finances. When pressed, a few years ago turned out to be 1986. When he asked if anything had changed in our firm in the interim, I had to stifle my instinct to answer, "Everything but my phone number." When I suggested he might want to come in to talk, he said he was going away for a while and would call me again. I found this conversation odd. It reinforced my feeling that some people like to check in every once in a while, like to know that you are still there in case they ever have the urge to see you, but intend to do nothing at present. Somehow your presence reassures them, and that is all they need.

Clunker Number Two—Will See You in Court. One of my colleagues called to recommend a client, but she added that the client came with a warning. The client was currently suing three major brokerage firms and her last financial advisor for alleged mistakes they had made in her account. Now her needs were simple. She wanted someone who would give straightforward advice that she could act on. I thanked my colleague for thinking of me, and told her I did not feel right even meeting this prospect, let alone working with her. You would not have taken her as a client, either, would you? If someone is so unhappy accepting advice, and has a history of disagreements, firings, lawsuits, and other nasty business, you could be next in court. At the very least, this client will be hard to please and take up too much of your time. At the worst, this client will embroil you in costly lawsuits. This behavior serves the client's need to rebel against authority figures. Defend yourself up front by not taking this client, even if you are desperate for new business.

Clunker Number Three—A Dysfunctional Family. There is nothing worse than to witness a family disagreeing loudly and angrily—and looking as if they will come to fisticuffs—around your conference table. Parents and siblings or even spouses can be so far apart in their financial thinking and so hung up on old family issues that they accuse, blame, cry, threaten, and shout at each other. To make matters worse, they seem to enjoy exhibiting this behavior in front of an audience (that is your role if you take them on, but if you are not available, they will perform this ritual in front of your staff or other clients). Whether they are exhibitionists with a need to act out in public, or they need to demand attention to feel important, or they simply are dysfunctional families with rude behavior, they will contribute more to the decibel level in your office than to the growth and success of your business. They do not really want your help because they are accustomed to the destructive patterns of their lives. If they refuse to modify their behavior, they are not a good match for your business.

Clunker Number Four—Unrealistic Expectations. Recently, I interviewed a retired woman who told me she could no longer live the way she used to. Her income was made up of Social Security and withdrawals from her portfolio. Her cost of living necessitated that this amount should be $35,000 per year from her portfolio. Her entire portfolio, which she wanted me to invest "with absolutely no risk" was currently $220,000. She expected her portfolio to support her through 25 years of retirement, and to grow as well. I sympathized with her desire to maintain her former lifestyle, but considered her expectations unrealistic. I tried to educate her about risk and return, about leaving money in the account so it could be reinvested, and about settling on a more realistic cost of living for her retirement years. However, she did not want to hear that her goals were unrealistic; she wanted to magically return to her former means and lifestyle. If a client's goals are unattainable, the best you can do is try to educate her, and encourage her to rework her goals. If you decide to take her on as a client, be forewarned that you will not be able to make her happy, and you probably will not be happy either.

mumbled something about his being hard to work with. I thought he was a nervous but fine gentleman, so I engaged him as a client. I should have called his last advisor directly. Client X took more of my time than 10 other clients I worked with combined. He e-mailed me insulting, angry notes almost daily. When he came in, he was always calm, polite, and friendly—then the computer blitz would resume. This client needed to dislike anyone who would work with him, just as Groucho Marx did not want to belong to any club that would admit him.

For two years, I thought about firing Client X, but restrained myself because of his lovely wife, and because I told myself he was not always so bad. But he was. He distracted me from my other clients, bewildered me, and required too much of my time. Finally, after I told him several times on the phone that perhaps he would be happier somewhere else, he left and became a client of a colleague of mine who I really like. I hate to think of the disruption he is likely to cause there. I have told my colleague that this client is a handful, and I am keeping my distance, waiting for two or so years to pass and for him to change firms again. After a few more changes, my colleagues and I can start a Do Not Work with Client X club.

I know several planners who at the end of each fiscal year fire their most time-consuming client of the year, and others who fire the five clients who give them the lowest revenues each year. Think of it as spring-cleaning. I do not routinely fire clients, and actually am loyal to my clients to the point of trying to repair bad relations for years before resorting to firing as the last chance to set a problem right. That is why I am more careful about who I will accept as a new client and think of each prospect as a potential match for my firm.

My firm has established a "Three strikes and you're out" rule. I will see what I call recurring prospects (those who keep coming back without making up their minds to go ahead with the work) three times, typically over a period of many years, and after that I will not allow them to return to my office even though they have usually done nothing in the interim and their need for professional assistance is increasingly great. Included in this tally are prospective clients who change their initial appointment three or more times, each time giving a credible excuse, but never actually showing up. Undoubtedly, they are thinking of me, and want me to continue to think of them. I am now considering reducing my rule to "Two strikes and you're out." These kinds of clients always sound so needy and convincing on the phone, but my experience tells me they generally do not work out as clients. People who cannot make up their minds the first two times, or are such dyed-in-the-wool procrastinators, need a very serious financial crisis to spur them to action.

The more combative clients speak for themselves, usually both loud and clear. Take them only if you are a glutton for punishment.

Be Sure You Have Covered This in the First Telephone Conversation

If the conversation is going well, you will want to schedule an in-person meeting to take the beginning relationship to the next level. To ease the transition, be sure to address the following before you end the phone call:

What does the prospect hope to accomplish in the first meeting?

What do you expect to accomplish?

When will the appointment be?

Where will it be?

Is the prospect bringing a relative or advisor?

Who will be there from your office?

What documents should the prospect bring?

Directions to your office (have them ready to discuss or to send)

Note: Never hang up without taking down a phone number where you can reach the prospect if a change in your appointment becomes necessary.

2

Sitting Down with Your Prospects: The Initial Consultation

Transitioning

If all goes well during the telephone conversation, and you establish some rapport, the prospect will want to take the next step, which is meeting with you. Unless this is geographically impossible, you should meet all new clients in person. You made a start in getting to know your prospective client over the phone, but nothing can replace an initial face-to-face meeting for setting the tone of your future relationship and for revealing the most private of your prospect's circumstances.

When you sit across from a prospect, you are more likely to discover her true feelings, goals, and needs than from phone calls and an exchange of documents through the mail. And the prospect will have a better chance to evaluate your services and see if you are on the same wavelength. If you are dealing with a couple, try to get both people to come in so that you get both points of view and can counter any resistance you sense from one of the parties. In-person meetings give you the chance to further assess the prospective client, determine what services she needs, show who you are, what you know, how you work, and what you can do.

Your Office as a Stage Set

My husband, who is also my partner, calls our office (specifically the reception area where all new clients and prospective clients wait to meet us) a Hollywood set. He means that we have taken the trouble to graphically project our style for all newcomers— and active clients—visiting our office to see.

Setting the stage is very important, since prospects can size up your surroundings in the first 30 seconds upon entering your office. Therefore, if your reception area is littered with papers, the carpet is torn, or the walls are stained, you must work long and hard to change the perception that you have a messy, disorganized firm. Showing off a deteriorating office is as bad as attending a meeting in dirty, frayed shirtsleeves. If you would not do one, you should not do the other.

I had a decorator help me achieve the look I wanted. Much of my firm's furniture is rich mahogany, some of the carpets are Oriental rugs, the fabrics are silks and silk blends, the paint is clean, and the lighting is clear and bright. I feel that entering my office is similar to visiting the personal library or den of a well-to-do businessperson. My office purposely feels part home, and so suggests comfort and nurture, and part professional, and so suggests competency and up-to-date business methods. I try to set a busy but gracious atmosphere, so clients see that my firm is professional yet thoughtful.

There are many options for offices today. You can make a nice arrangement of very modern pieces, have all employees in an open area, or use a separate (non-living) area of your home. Simple utilitarian pieces that hold the tools of your trade can convey a straightforward, efficient use of time. Find the style that fits your personality and your budget. Remember that your surroundings offer clues about your style and your business practices. Are you organized or thumbing through papers every time a client visits? A well-maintained filing system can convey that you are responsible. A stylish arrangement of furniture suggests that you are up-to-date. Comfortable seating shows that you care about your clients. Be sure that your surroundings project the message you wish clients to receive.

Stage Set Components

Waiting area

Information about you and your services

Beverage and snack

Bright lights

Cheeriness

Well-maintained setting

Private meeting space

Quiet/calm

When I greet a client, I like to feel as if I am meeting someone at the door to my home. You can accomplish this feeling in your personal space within a large company with touches that express your style, or as the sole practitioner of a small business.

A reception area can be as large as a room or as small as the doorway into your office. In my reception area—which at one time was two chairs just feet away from my desk but now is a separate room—I have always placed articles about the principals of my firm that have appeared in the press, my company brochure, and other business-related literature. Recently, my teenage son, who played high school football, was in a sports article in my local paper. As a proud parent, I added a copy of the article to my waiting-room paraphernalia. What do you think clients and prospective clients have commented on the most since? I believe the article about my son allows them to see me as a total person, with interests similar to theirs, as well as a professional. It also gives them entry to discuss their families and their own personal situations. For those who are not sports-minded, I also display paintings made by my daughter, who is a professional artist, on my walls. That has led to many interesting personal discussions as well. Not surprising, many of my clients are artists. We seem to have an instinctive rapport.

In your office, your seating arrangements, your personal mementos such as trinkets from a recent trip or hobby and personal photos, and your professional credentials, perhaps diplomas and awards displayed on a credibility wall (see the following section), will all speak about who you are and what style you wish to establish. One advisor I know is a sailing enthusiast and has pictures of his boat and awards from races he won in his office. Another keeps a picture of himself and his two-year-old grandson playing fire chief, both wearing firemen hats, on his desk. If you have a hobby or a collection, put a few representative pieces on your bookshelves. If you have children or grandchildren, put their pictures on your desk. If you have taken interesting trips, keep some mementos around. Do not underestimate the importance of expressing your personal side. And the cheerful, happy-to-see-you greeting you convey with a smile and a strong handshake can get you off to the right start.

The Credibility Wall

Creating your office is akin to establishing a comfort zone, a place where clients can be themselves, share their most personal thoughts and circumstances, and not be fearful of judgment or criticism. They should know that they are in a no-combat zone from your attitude, furnishings, greeting, and credentials.

Much as when you visit a doctor for the first time and glance at his diplomas, everything in your office should signal solidness, stability, experience, integrity, comfort, and compassion. One ingredient in presenting yourself as a caring professional is your credibility wall. That is a space that holds your credentials and lends credibility to your advice. On this wall, always within the client's sight, should be your educational diplomas, membership in professional societies, and honors and awards received.

This credibility wall helps prospective clients know they have come to the right place. If you are starting out and have yet to amass many credentials, it is okay to start small. A nicely framed college diploma and a membership in one or two professional societies are a good beginning. You can add to your wall over time.

If you have press articles quoting you, they can be on the wall as well, or on a second credibility wall in your reception area, as they are in my office, where prospective clients have the time to read articles and get to know your somewhat less formal professional side. As a last resort, if you are faced with an empty space, frame relevant financial and investment articles that may interest your clients and hang them on the wall. At least these articles will indicate that you are aware of your clients' concerns and you and they are starting off on the same page.

You can also convey credibility through your actions. Visual materials can be useful here. I know one colleague who does a drop-dead computer presentation for each prospect who walks in the door. I cannot imagine anyone leaving without signing up after being dazzled by the latest graphic tools. However, nothing beats a personal tour of your office, an introduction to the members of your staff, and deeply felt interest in the prospect's personal situation.

You can present yourself as an advocate for your clients, either in specific situations (e.g., meeting with their accountant), or in a more general (we will take care of your financial needs) sense. If they want to be educated about finances, that is a role you can volunteer to assume.

Of course, you cannot expect to capture all prospects as clients, nor should you want to. You should concentrate on those with whom you have genuine rapport and for whom you think you can offer real value. Think about whether you want to present yourself as an all-purpose planner or whether you wish to identify your niche and communicate who you like to work with and what you do best.

The In-Office Meeting Agenda

Over the years, I have developed an understanding of what people want to discuss when they come to see me, and how to make the transition from sympathetic stranger to trusted advisor. I want my prospective clients to know what to expect when they come in. Therefore, I developed a handout that I usually mail to people before the meeting, but can hand out in the waiting area if time is short (see sidebar "Our Initial Consultation"). At my firm, the emphasis is always on the prospective client and his concerns, needs, and goals.

Our Initial Consultation

The purpose of this meeting is to discuss your major financial concerns and determine how to address them most effectively. It is a first step in setting financial goals and building the mutual trust and rapport that are so important in an advisor-client relationship. We find that providing you with a first-meeting agenda helps us focus on the most important issues and use this time productively.

Here is a typical agenda:

- Fill out a short questionnaire that clarifies your purpose in seeking financial advice.

- Tell us about yourself—for example, your stage of life, current financial situation, needs for today, and goals for the future.

- Discuss portfolio statements, tax returns, and relevant financial documents that you bring to the meeting.

- Ask us questions. We recommend you prepare a list of the most important ones. We will prioritize these items in our discussion.

- Discuss how we can work with you, our investment approach, and your goals and risk tolerance.

- Be sure we have addressed your major concerns and have fully described our services.

- Be certain that you understand how we can help you fulfill your financial goals.

- Discuss fully the service we recommend for you, show you samples of our work, provide you with names of references, and describe our fee structure.

We look forward to meeting you.

Of course, now that you have put it in writing, aroused your prospects' curiosity, and given a framework to the meeting, you must follow your agenda closely. Start with cues you picked up on the phone. Ask your prospective clients about themselves; give them a chance to ask you questions. Discuss how you can work together. Address their major concerns. Show them samples of your work, and discuss your fees.

Finally, to make your first meeting go smoothly, if you asked the prospect to bring documents or complete a questionnaire, refer to those pieces of information at the meeting, even if it is just to look at the adjusted gross income line on a tax return or to acknowledge that they have more stocks than bonds in a brokerage account. You do not want your prospective clients to feel they wasted their time gathering documents or are not being taken seriously. In other words, if you ask for it, and you get it, use it.

Overcoming Prospects' Fears

New clients often come to this first meeting with some trepidation. Perhaps they feel that they have not done all they could with their financial decisions. Or they may worry that other people have saved more than they did. They may feel ignorant about financial matters. Just recently, I spoke to a young woman who said she was too embarrassed to tell me the size of her portfolio because it was so small. After I coaxed her, she admitted to a high five-figure portfolio, certainly nothing to be ashamed of.

There is no right or wrong figure for a portfolio, but people's expectations are often greater than their bank accounts. Celebrities who are in the news are usually much wealthier than people our clients know personally, and give clients a skewed vision of where they should be financially. It is your job to bring clients back to reality.

Making people comfortable is where the stage set concept comes into play. You want to put people at ease before they even meet you. At my firm, prospects wait for their initial appointment—but never for more than a few minutes—amid representations of our work and the recognition we have received. They are greeted by a receptionist who drops what she is doing and turns her complete attention to them. She takes their coats, offers them a beverage, and engages them in conversation until it is time for their meeting.

This is something you can do even if you are on your own. When my firm was smaller, I paid the same attention to making clients feel welcome. For years, I was the official greeter; then, as the firm grew, I scheduled appointments only when my then part-time assistant was available. Now I have a full-time greeter ready to extend a welcome on behalf of the firm.

To set the tone for the meeting, the receptionist hands prospective clients a one-page form to complete. I want to learn about new prospects, but I do not want to pressure them. They are asked a few brief questions that encourage them to think about why they came, which helps me begin the conversation when we meet and sets them at ease. The initial meeting questionnaire below differs from the information gathered during the phone call, which covered a small amount of information about their situation. The questionnaire asks specifically about their motivation, their concerns, what made them think about financial planning, who referred them to me, the goals they have for our first meeting, and the relationship they hope to establish with an advisor. It begins to place financial planning in its proper perspective, as part of their lives. It also serves as a good reminder for me once they leave, so good, in fact, that I staple it to the inside cover of each client's file.

The answers I receive most frequently tell me that people are looking for a knowledgeable advisor who is trustworthy and can communicate well with them. In other words, my prospective clients want to be taken seriously, and they value a good, honest relationship as much as they do financial experience or skills.

First Meeting Questionnaire

Date _____

Name _____

Address _____

Phone _____

1. How did you hear of L.J. Altfest & Co., Inc.?

2. What motivated you to seek financial advice?

3. What qualities are you looking for in an advisor?

4. What do you hope to get out of our meeting today?

To date, no one has ever objected to answering these few questions. Some people whiz through them; others take considerable time. Most couples choose one person to answer; others prefer to write their own respective responses or consult before answering together. Only twice have I been asked for a second form so that each spouse could complete his or her own copy. Both times I attempted to dissuade them—I think it is important since they came together and hope to resolve their problems together for them to start out (literally) on the same page.

Each question in the questionnaire has a purpose. The first leads prospects to recall the connection between us. If a good friend or trusted advisor recommended me, they are sure to have confidence in my services. The second asks them to focus on their situation and begin to articulate their concerns. The third question brings to mind many qualities of training, experience, and character that I am sure I can provide. Finally, the fourth question leads prospective clients to focus on a goal for our first meeting that is hopefully realistic. That is, most say they want an understanding of what I can do for them, or information about my fees. Few expect me to solve their financial problems on the spot.

The answers my form generates are very revealing.

Question 1—How Did You Hear of . . . ? Knowing who referred a client to you provides a starting point for your conversation, and reminds the prospect of the connection that led him to you. It is a safe place to begin to learn about each other before delving into more personal topics.

Question 2—What Motivated You . . . ? Usually their motivations come from major life changes, such as death of a loved one, birth of a child, approaching retirement, nearing a major birthday, a significant promotion, marriage, divorce, a legal settlement, or inheritance. This shows that people will generally coast along as they always have until they are propelled into action by a major change that leaves them uncertain about what to do.

Question 3—What Qualities Are You . . . ? Most frequent answers include the ability to communicate effectively, knowledge, insight, compassion, patience, and help making the right decisions. Another frequent answer is integrity and synonyms for this quality, such as honesty and trustworthiness. This indicates that people want someone they can trust who will point them in the right direction and care about their progress.

Question 4—What Do You Hope to Get out of . . . ? Prospective clients want to leave your office with a sense of how they might work with you, your fees, references from some of your clients, and the beginning of a long-term relationship. The answer to this last question is extremely telling. Your prospects want a comfortable place where they can discuss their concerns not just as another impersonal problem to be solved, but in a continuing personal relationship between two mature, caring adults who will solve problems together, even if it is you doing the solving on their behalf.

Comments that catch my attention include those that indicate a desire for a customized strategy, something I would do expressly for one client alone, not for everyone who walks through my door. Others have asked for focused attention, availability, and a nonpatronizing attitude, indicating again the wish for a highly personal, specialized, caring relationship. One prospect wrote that he wanted to "test our chemistry." Who said establishing a financial planning relationship was unlike dating? A blind date and an initial consultation have this in common: They are both an opportunity to determine if you feel good with a person and decide if you have common interests and wish to ever see that person again.

What can you learn from this questionnaire? It is very important that you find a way to convince your prospects of your overriding interest in them and their situations. I go out of my way to do this by focusing on their concerns from the first meeting forward. They receive my full attention when they visit and when they call. I am even willing to take extra steps to resolve their issues. I have arranged meetings with three generations of a family, and have moderated meetings with clients' other advisors. If you give 100 percent of yourself, you will have happy clients.

I reassure my prospective clients that this quiz is not the SATs and will not be graded by my staff. It is used simply to begin the discussion process and get people thinking about why they came and what they want to talk about. Intimidating your prospects would not be constructive. The initial questionnaire is just a jumping-off prop to begin to know each other personally and professionally.

Comfort for the Stomach and the Spirit

I always offer my guests some comfort food. For some prospects, coming to see you is a stressful situation. To help soothe my clients, I keep coffee, tea, sodas, and bottled water on hand. I also have either fruit, candies, or cookies available. If a meeting goes past lunchtime, I offer to send out for sandwiches. If you had the type of mother who consoled you when things were not going your way by baking cookies, you will remember how comforting certain foods are. And it can make your clients feel well taken care of. With a small amount of petty cash and just a little effort, you can be caring, thoughtful, and comforting.

I serve cookies on china plates, fruit in crystal bowls, and take the time to brew coffee for my clients. I believe my extra effort is duly noted and appreciated by visitors to my office. I also like to keep a pitcher of water and glasses nearby. Even if the offer of something to drink is initially refused, water is likely to be appreciated if the meeting stretches on.

Two Planners Can Be Better Than One

When I meet prospective clients, I prefer to have another planner with me in the room. Typically, but not always, the other planner is a man so we represent both sexes, and sometimes the other planner is of a different age. That way, we can act as a check on each other, get two different points of view about the situation, and compare notes after the meeting. We can keep the conversation flowing, and generate ideas during the interview. We are sure to cover all the bases.

Most important, including two people of different genders or ages in the meeting increases the chance of relating to the client on some level. This works particularly well when there is a married couple or two or more other relatives in the meeting; then there is someone for each person to talk and relate to. For example, one planner can listen to a prospect's commentary on how hard it is to save money, while the other planner can discuss investment risk.

Someone once told me that he thought my planning practice was successful because there was a woman involved, and some clients like to talk to a woman. I would revise that to read "a well-trained, competent, sympathetic professional who is a good listener." It is worth repeating that I feel every prospect who enters my office has an important and interesting personal story to tell, and I do them the courtesy of listening. Because telling their story is often accompanied by intense emotion, I keep a box of tissues at the ready, and give prospective clients my full attention.

I believe it inspires confidence in the client to sit across the table from a professional married couple or from colleagues who respect each other and work well together. It establishes a mood that is conducive to relating personal information and knowing it is being received in a personal yet professional way, which leads to a full, rich discussion.

If you are a one-person office, your ability to listen to the prospective client, observe body language, and ignore all phones, computers, faxes, and other distractions will be crucial to the development of a business relationship. Repeating and summarizing what the prospective client tells you is a very effective technique. It lets clients know that you have heard their concerns, and are preparing to respond to them. It also gives you a chance to correct any inconsistencies you may have heard. In addition, as a one-person office, you have a distinct advantage that you can stress to prospective clients: You will be the one doing the work, taking their calls, and giving them your personal attention.

A written list of questions or topics you wish to cover can help you get to know your prospects well beyond the preliminary conversation you had on the telephone. Many personal circumstances and intense emotions are best suited for the in-person meeting. My list includes, but is not limited to:

How old are you?

Where do you work?

What do you do?

How long have you been there?

How much do you earn?

How much do you save or dissave?

Are you married?

What does your spouse do?

Do you have or expect to have children?

If your children are grown, are they self-supporting?

In an ideal world, what would you like to achieve financially?

Do you have a will?

Are there likely to be any inheritances in your future?

From these basic facts, you can proceed to more substantive issues, such as the person's financial concerns. Of course, the idea is not to launch a rapid-fire assault, but rather to cover all these bases in a natural conversation over the course of the meeting.

Do Not Be Judgmental or Critical
(What! You Are 49 and You Have Not Planned!)

I have heard confidences from very successful (and occasionally famous) people that would certainly make it into the *National Enquirer.* I have heard that a husband is filing for divorce before his wife knows. I have heard that a family is broke and have been asked not to tell other members. I have learned of unsavory family characters, ne'er-do-well children, even abusive relatives. I have been told about financial doings that sound somewhat sleazy (we always send those people on their way), but I never criticize, act horrified, or express disapproval. I certainly never laugh at anyone or think them stupid (although many of my clients tell me they are "idiots," "know nothing about money," are "financially illiterate," or have "blown it"). That is not my job. My job is simply to help people do better than they have been doing.

To the parents of a 16 year old who come to see me to "plan" for college education in one year, I never say, "You should have come here 10 years ago." Rather, I may help them search for financial aid. Similarly, when a recently retired man came to tell me he had stopped working a month previous and knew he should have come to see me one month earlier, I did not say, "You should have come here 15 or 20 years ago while we still had time to make a difference." I helped him determine all his assets and sources of income, his living expenses, and decide how he could close the gap between the two.

I truly am never shocked at any lack of planning because I believe I could have done that myself except for a few turns on the paths of life I chose. My advice to you if you do hear something that surprises you is to first pause by taking a drink of water or take a deep breath, and then forge ahead to help your client plan to do better in the future. Dwelling on the past is no more productive during an initial interview in your office than it generally is in other parts of your client's life.

Selling Yourself

In a first meeting, you have a wonderful opportunity to show off your skills, knowledge, and concern and to present yourself as the prospect's best alternative. Your prospect may be interviewing many planners, or you may be the only one. Most people will tell you if they are interviewing other professionals.

Some planners like to be the first one the prospect meets in an attempt to make a strong initial impression. Others ask prospects to visit them last, so they can respond to any challenges from their competitors. I do not know if it makes a difference whether you are first or last. What is significant is maximizing this one-on-one opportunity to present yourself as their best alternative.

On the plus side, you have a near-captive audience in the room with you. Be prepared to differentiate your firm from other firms, your style from that of other planners, and to set your personal skills way above the rest of the pack. You can do that by highlighting your own strengths. Always avoid bad-mouthing the competition. When a prospect asks me what I think about another firm, I generally say, "I do not know much about the way they work, but here is how we would work with you." Of course, if the competition is someone I really do know well, I might add

What Sets Your Firm Apart

Age of Firm	_____
Location	_____
Background	_____
Experience	_____
Education	_____
Unusual Expertise	_____
Staff Members	_____
Foreign Languages	_____
Client Niche	_____
Specialty	_____
Services	_____

that they are a fine firm, and then explain how we would work with that person.

If you have not thought about what you can offer that your competitors do not, take the time to do it now.

One planner I know only takes clients from her own prep-school background, thereby developing a niche that other planners may not have access to. Another offers to speak to clients in Spanish, French, or English, whatever makes them more comfortable. Still another stresses his background as a dentist in a previous career, and works mainly with dentists. Others see people from their country of origin.

When you attend financial conferences and listen to your colleagues, in what ways do you feel different from your peers? What sets you apart? What do you offer that others do not? Think about developing those special traits and come up with a two-minute summary of your special attributes to market your practice.

Providing the Right Amount of Feedback

It is important that your prospective clients sense you are interested in them personally and in their financial situation. While it may not be necessary to offer an "um-hmm" after every com-ment, paying attention, asking appropriate questions, and main-taining eye contact are ways to establish a good relationship. Sometimes even a nod of your head will convince the prospect that you are concentrating all your attention on him and it is safe to continue.

If you have a question you always ask and your prospect is dis-cussing another topic, do not interrupt his train of thought. Doing so may make you appear disinterested in something that is important to him. Jot down your question, and let him con-tinue. The best approach is to join in *his* conversation, by listen-ing, questioning, agreeing (only when you feel you legitimately can), or nodding your head in interest.

Pay attention to the prospect's body language. One prospect who came into my office refused to take off her coat through the whole 90-minute meeting. This resistance was mirrored in her close-lipped conversation, in which she offered very little per-sonal information, and mouthed only a "yes" or "no" in response to my questions. When at the end of the session she had not begun to relax, I knew we would never have an open relationship.

At times, you can adjust your behavior to that of the prospect. I do not believe it is necessary to mimic the behavior of your prospects, for example crossing your legs if they cross theirs, or leaning your chin on your hand when they do. Yet do respond to body signals. For example, one client came in with his arms folded across his chest, a very defensive posture. I knew I had an ambivalent prospect in front of me, and allowed more time for warm-up before getting to substantive fact-finding. It took half an hour of small talk, chatting about where the prospect lives, his children's careers, and his grandchildren's accomplishments for him to relax and be more forthcoming in our conversation.

Most of all, prospective clients want your undivided interest. Plan your time with a minimum of interruptions and devote your full attention to the task at hand.

The "T" Word—Trust

Up until now, I have discussed steps to make people feel com-fortable with you on the phone and in your office. Clients want to know that you are concerned about them, that you will give them your attention, your care, and your best advice. The third item on my initial consultation questionnaire asks what qualities the prospect would most like to have in an advisor. Trust leads the list, beyond all other attributes.

My clients ask me about trust in many ways. They want to know that they can trust me to consider their interests first, protect their privacy, do my best work on their behalf, and treat them with respect. They would like to think that their concerns are serious to me.

On one level, they ask me obvious and professional questions as a way of gauging whether I am going about things the right way. They want to know what professional societies I belong to, how long I have been in business, and whether I have experience with clients like them. They ask if I am a registered investment advisor and whether I have appropriate training and designations.

Once they cover these basics, clients get to their more personal and deeply felt issues. Here are some typical questions, and what they may really mean:

Will I always be able to talk to you?	*Will I be important to you?*
Will you return my calls promptly?	*Are you likely to take me seriously?*
Will you be doing my work yourself?	*How much effort will you put into our relationship?*
Do you keep my information confidential?	*Will we have a personal and private relationship?*
Will you call me if anything happens that I should know about?	*Will you think of me from time to time?*
What will I do if you retire?	*Will you abandon me while I still need you?*

Notice that experience, education, and even good advice all take a back seat to trust. Think of your own experience going to an attorney to draw up your will. If you are like most people, you probably want someone who you can confide personal feelings in, tell information you want kept confidential, and who will give you the same good advice she would give a member of her own family. If you do not trust your lawyer, you may not take her advice, you may need to get second and third opinions, and you may change legal advisors after a short period of time. Basically, in your relationships with legal professionals, you want to know that you have chosen your advisors well and that you are doing the best you can for yourself.

Your clients want the same. If you do not have their confidence, they will screen all your advice, compare it with other advisors, and filter your information through their own years of experience. They may not act on your recommendations. Your relationship will be tenuous at best. It is really quite simple to establish yourself as a trusted advisor. Do what you say you will in a timely fashion, keep confidences private, always take your clients seriously, act in your clients' best interests, and be professional and ethical in all you do. Then you will earn the trust of clients and colleagues alike, and be more likely to keep your clients for life.

Beginning the Process

Helping Clients Set Goals

Working with a client without goals is like driving a car without fuel. It may sputter along for a short while, but eventually you are going to run out of gas. Goals are the fuel that drives your client's car. It is one of your primary responsibilities to probe during the initial meeting for your client's goals.

I find out about my clients' goals in three ways: the direct method, the indirect method, and by assignment. Using the direct method, I ask clients, "What motivated you to come to my office?," "What do you hope to accomplish?," "What are your financial concerns?," and "Where would you like to be 5 or 10 or 20 years from now?" Some clients know themselves well and answer with certainty; others respond as if this is the first time they ever thought about such things, sputtering along like cars without gas. These clients need my help articulating their goals.

When using the indirect method, I listen carefully to what my clients tell me the first time and in subsequent meetings for clues about their goals. Sometimes I write down what my clients say word for word so that when I am analyzing their situation, I can remember what was most important to them. Recently, clients have told me, "I do not want to worry about money like my mother did" (translation: I would like to save more money now so that I am comfortable in my later years), "I am not sure that I want to stay in my job past 50" (translation: please tell me when and how I can achieve financial independence), "We are notorious for putting things off" (translation: We are getting started late in life and need your guidance), and "I am sure I will die at a young age, so I want my wife and two small children to be well provided for" (translation: either health issues, recent loss of a loved one, or a pessimistic personality suggest that I may die early, so estate planning is a primary goal). I take all these goals into account and over time piece them together into a meaningful patchwork that gives us, the client and me, a direction that we can work toward.

My third method, the assignment, takes the form of a questionnaire that all clients take home after the first meeting. My questionnaire has two columns, one for each spouse in a marriage, or each partner in a personal (but not necessarily legally binding) relationship to express their goals, priorities, family situation, feelings about investment risk, income, and expenses. To lighten the mood and underline the importance of the work, I tell my clients that this is their homework.

My questionnaire delves into client goals in several ways, moving from overall goals to very specific ones. I ask clients to list goals, embellish them, and then prioritize them. To establish goals you can work with, you may have to educate your clients that not all goals can be achieved at once.

Finally, I supply my clients' four most frequently stated goals and leave room for respondents to contribute some of their own:

Improving your current standard of living   _____

Enjoying a comfortable retirement   _____

Building or providing an estate for your heirs   _____

Educating your children   _____

Any other goals that are important to you   _____

I then ask the client to prioritize those goals from 1 (highest) to 5 (lowest), based in order of importance.

Discussing goals is a means of bringing to the conscious mind and to my attention important issues that are not always immediately apparent, even to the client. It helps clarify for you and your clients what they really value. Recently, a couple in their forties told me they had no children and did not expect to have any. Yet on the goals list they placed educating children as their third most important goal. Puzzled, I asked them what they meant by that response. It turned out that one spouse still thought having children was a possibility, and did not want to completely close the door by not planning for that likelihood. My questions led the couple to negotiate their life goals rather than bury them. Once goals are on the table, you and your clients can decide how to deal with them.

Personal Financial Goals and Objectives—Points from My Client Questionnaire

Financial goals are sometimes hard to articulate. Objectives such as faster asset growth, paying lower taxes, and protecting assets against inflation are common concerns of most individuals. These are not only financial goals. They also impact your current and future lifestyle. How do you imagine your finances over the next several years? What do you expect your retirement lifestyle to be like? Review your specific situation—current lifestyle considerations, family needs, feelings about risk and investments, alternative career and life plans, health, desired gifts or inheritances to family members, heirs, etc.—and try to review your goals.

This is only a start. We will help you further define and clarify your goals and their financial implications. Please use the next few pages to comment on your goals, their relative priorities to each other, when you hope to reach these goals, and their cost in today's dollars. You may want to have a discussion, take some notes, or reflect before you begin this section. Although we do not expect you to plan your entire future, knowledge of your hopes and expectations can help us work toward a scenario that is appropriate and comfortable for you. Feel free to use additional pages if you need more space.

(Continued)

Client I's goals:

Client II's goals:

Now quantify some of your goals by responding to the following questions:

What do you consider your primary financial goal or concern over the next three years?

Over the next 5 to 10 years? Beyond 10 years?

What is your most desired standard of living?

At what age would you like to be able to retire?

What is your desired after-tax retirement income estimated in today's dollars?

Would you consider moving to a smaller home or condo, or relocating after retirement?

How much would that home cost?

Do you have any other concerns or questions about retirement?

Do you have other financial goals you hope to achieve?

(Reprinted with permission from Mary Malgoire and David Drucker.)

Fleshing Out the Goals

Once you know the goals, you have to translate them into financial terms, and examine the parameters of each one. For example, when clients tell me they want to buy a house, it is my job to determine first how much house they would like to buy, and second whether that goal is attainable. I sometimes ask directly how much house they would like, or else I ask them if they have looked at any houses, or whether they have checked out the real-estate ads in the neighborhood of their choice and can tell me how much their desired house will cost.

The same holds true for other goals. If they want to plan to educate two children, it is important to know whether there will be educational costs prior to college, whether college will be private or public, whether they expect to finance four years for each child or graduate school as well, and whether they are comfortable with their children contributing part of the costs either through earnings, loans, gifts, or not at all. If a client wants a new car, I ask what car and which features he is considering. Planning for a Volkswagen Beetle may be attainable, while planning for a Jaguar with all the trimmings may not.

Once I can set parameters and place goals in a financial framework through knowing the item, the cost, and the timing, I can consider the likelihood of achieving each goal.

Getting to Know Themselves

It is your job to draw your clients out, get them to think about things that may be uncomfortable, and come to conclusions about their lives they may never have confronted before. You have already taken steps in this direction by working with them to establish their goals. Do not feel shy about asking your clients questions; it is a necessary part of your job. Do not think of it as prying, but as performing your due diligence, that is, getting to know the needs of each client before you begin the job. This is an area in which you can add real value.

A psychologist who is a client of mine tells me that her clients will talk to her about everything but money. They will not let her be privy to that part of their lives. But they do talk to me about their money situation. I know because she sends her patients with money issues to my office.

Ask your clients how comfortable they are in their jobs, how secure their careers are, how long-lasting their personal relationships will be. Discuss when they hope to retire, whether they expect to have more children, and if they will have to provide for loved ones at some point. These are the kinds of questions that you should raise with your clients right from the beginning. If you seem genuinely interested in them and in their lives, clients will be direct and not feel that your personal questions are inappropriate.

You need a full and accurate account of your client's personal life in order to plan effectively. There is no point in assuming that a client who earns $100,000 a year will continue to earn that much if the client secretly contemplates giving it all up to go back to school. Nor is there much point doing college planning for a couple with two children if they have not told you they are about to adopt a third child. I like the gentle but outright approach. I always ask my clients about their ODD FISH:

Occupation

Domicile

Debt

Family

Inheritance

Secret wishes

Hobbies

Each of these topics should help you travel down a path to more complete knowledge about your client. *Occupation* is important because it gives you background information about the client's skills, interests, career path, current earnings and future earning possibilities, likelihood of remaining in a particular geographic location, and so on. *Domicile* will tell you how your client is living now and his ideal way of living in the future. In many areas, the decision whether to buy or rent is an important topic. Talking to your older clients about trading down on their home in retirement can be useful. I always discuss *debt* with my clients so I can learn about their spending habits and assess if they are living within their means. I separate debt into one-time-only debt (e.g., refurbishing a home or paying for a daughter's wedding), planned debt (e.g., for a house), and ongoing debt (e.g., a credit card debt).

Talking about *family* can lead you down many interesting roads. You can get to know your clients on a more personal level and hear their concerns about elderly parents, dependent siblings, and raising, educating, and leaving an inheritance to their children. I always ask clients about future *inheritances,* because I have noticed that some people plan their lives counting on some day having an inheritance, while others choose to ignore any possibility of inheriting and rely solely on their own means. Since so many people are living into their nineties today, I even ask clients in their sixties and seventies if they might have an inheritance in their future.

Knowing your clients' *secret wishes* and *hobbies* can add a new dimension to their financial stories. When they share their dreams with you, the relationship becomes truly personal. Dreams and hobbies such as buying a boat, joining a country club, retiring early, or having a vacation home all have a financial aspect to them.

A truly good discussion on just these few topics can easily go on for one to two hours. Each answer can engender further questions. For example, once you know what your client does on the job, you can ask about income, bonuses, expected increases, job security, and her desire to remain in the job. You can then ask those same questions about her spouse's career. Finally, you can find out when they expect to retire from their occupations.

Just recently, I had the following conversation with Ned and Louise:

KCA: What do you do, Ned?

Ned: I develop computer software.

KCA: How long have you been doing that?

Ned: About 13 years.

KCA: What is your annual income at your job?

Ned: $65,000 and usually a $10,000 bonus.

KCA: It sounds pretty stable. Do you expect to stay there?

Ned: I think so, although two people in my company just left. We get lots of offers.

KCA: Louise, you work for a television network, right?

Louise: Right. I have been with the network for five years.

KCA: What is your current salary?

Louise: It is not a high-paying industry. I make $45,000.

KCA: Do you expect to remain in your job?

Louise: I would really like something with more flexible hours. I might leave in a year or two and start my own business, but I am not sure yet. Maybe we should not count on my salary continuing at this level for more than two years.

This brief conversation was very revealing. I learned the family occupations, work history, salaries, and the likelihood of future earnings. The couple themselves began to deal with issues of income level and possible career change. Until then, Louise never told Ned about her interest in leaving her position, and was afraid to bring up the possibility of not earning as much money in the future. This opened the pathway to more in-depth conversations about Ned and Louise's plans.

Note especially where your clients are now and any changes they expect to make. Although financial planning certainly documents a person's or a family's situation at a point in time, you do want to ascertain how long current conditions will likely apply. Just recently, I did a plan for Marcy, a woman with considerable debt and a young child to raise. We had met two months earlier. Knowing that people with cash management problems can easily eat up their savings cushion due to unexpected events, I asked Marcy whether she still had the $10,000 certificate of deposit she owned when we last met. I was not surprised to learn that Marcy had used $3,500 of that money to pay for medical care, and another $1,000 for her daughter's needs. This conversation led to Marcy's dilemma about whether to move to a lower-cost state. By asking just a few well-placed questions, I learned a lot of pertinent information and was able to revamp my advice and make it relevant to Marcy's current situation. Ask questions about change, even if it has never come up before with this particular client, keep a list of when changes might occur, and at what financial cost. You can explore these changes in greater detail when you begin your financial analysis.

Some of this information will turn up in your questionnaire, and some can be gleaned from your conversations. Before clients fill out my questionnaire, I assure them that if they have trouble, they can call with questions or even bring the questionnaire in and one of our professionals will sit down and go through it with them. The only thing I will not do is fill the questionnaire out with my own opinions for people who ask what I think they should answer to some question.

When clients say, "I do not know how much investment risk I am willing to take. That is what I came to you for," I tell them not to worry. We will work to arrive at the right risk tolerance for them together. But by speaking and thinking about my questions, and starting to answer as much as they can, they help me determine what is right for them. I have never yet said that there is no right (or wrong) answer because it seems obvious to me, but I think my reassurance to those few reluctant clients conveys my belief. When clients return the questionnaire, they frequently comment on how much they learned about themselves while going through this fact-finding process, and thank me for leading them to deeper self-knowledge.

Accepting Where They Are versus Moving Forward

To establish the basis for your working relationship, try to find out why your clients are in your office. One of my favorite questions is, "Tell me in your own words, What brings you here at this time?" Typically, clients tell me they are too busy to handle their own investments, they are getting older and do not feel they are keeping up as well anymore, or they have just had a major life change and need to know what to do.

Make a note of their reasons for coming to see you. It could be useful later on as you get to know more about their situations. One of my clients, Leslie, told me she was looking for a way to deal with her controlling father who had given her large amounts of money with considerable strings attached. That might have meant one of two things: Could Leslie, a mature woman, educate herself enough to handle her own finances and wean herself from her dad, or would I let her lean on me the way she leaned on her father, and make all her financial decisions for her? As our relationship evolved, it turned out Leslie wanted to improve her financial knowledge and take more responsibility for financial decisions, which is how I prefer to work with clients, so we formed a comfortable alliance.

Financial planning is an active process, and an interactive one as well. It is not just a portrait of someone's life, but an action plan agreed to and worked on by the planner and the client. I consider it my job to move clients from here and now to where they want to be. I look for solutions to their problems and ways to reach their goals. Sometimes, though, you have to start by accepting where clients are now, uncover the reasons they are in their current position, educate them to do better, and teach them that it may take a while to accomplish their dreams. For many people, it is easier to maintain the status quo than to actively make changes, even for the better. It is easier to let the certificate of deposit automatically renew every year than to open a brokerage account and invest in mutual funds. Similarly, it is easier to keep your old property and casualty insurance policy than to update it and keep it current. And it is easier to hang on to your old, out-of-date will than to make an appointment with an attorney to have it revised to fit your family's current situation. I have done everything short of taking clients by the hand to get them to update their situations.

Leslie and I had many conversations about her controlling father, her childhood, her relationships with siblings and with her father's new wife, and even at one point role-played discussing her choices with her dad. (I played the dad.) She practiced telling her dad she was grateful for his generosity, confronting him about taking responsibility for her own decisions from now on, and was eventually able to meet with him and gain his agreement to let her handle her own money, which he had managed until then. This was a sign of Leslie's growing confidence and a meaningful step for her to take. With some assistance and a boost to her self-confidence, Leslie prepared to move forward. We both felt good about the outcome.

What Would You Like If You Could Have Anything?

My final question, after I ferret out the measurable information, addresses my clients' dreams and wishes. This question requires special attention. It is the most open-ended of the questions, and is truly revealing about your client's hopes, wishes, personality, confidence, and perceptions. Note that this question differs from the goals question because goals are generally attainable, and in fact, your clients may already have taken steps to accomplish some of them, such as contributing to retirement plans at work.

The responses to this final question fit more into the category of wish list. In most cases, this question adds a new dimension to your client's planning, and puts all sorts of happy possibilities on the table. I have clients talk about buying vacation homes, going on great trips, taking early retirement, and helping their children. Talking about a client's wish list is similar to the technique of visualization. If you have attended professional conferences, you might have come across psychologists and coaches who tell you to imagine growing your business and picture what it would look like. Imagining it is supposed to make the goal more likely to materialize, and besides, it is fun to do. No one has ever told me that they cannot come up with any dreams.

Once you know the client's dreams, you can see which, if any, are possible to achieve either soon or over the long term. At the very least, you will have delved further into the client's psyche and know who you are dealing with.

My Accordion Concept: Minimum, Merely Satisfactory, and Most Lavish Goals

Very often, when a person's income increases, so do her lifestyle expenses. It is easy to increase the cost of living and spend up. It is not quite as easy to decrease the cost of living or spend down when things are not going so well. I view my clients' spending habits as expandable, like an accordion. When times are flush, their living style expands; when times are lean, their living style contracts. What you need to determine with your clients is the least, the merely satisfactory, and the most lavish lifestyle in many categories that they can adjust to.

One client of mine told me he was buying a car for his teenage son, and not just a car, but a four-wheel drive SUV that would set him back about $36,000 before extras, maintenance, insurance, and parking. We discussed his young son's responsibility for the purchase as well as his needs. We decided that $36,000 was a hefty chunk of change for that family, and my client went home to discuss what other car would satisfy his son. It turned out that the SUV was his son's most lavish goal; his merely satisfactory goal, a new American car that would meet all his needs, cost considerably less both in purchase price and insurance costs. The son's minimum goal was a used Japanese car at considerably lower cost.

The client decided on his son's merely satisfactory car, and as an added benefit from their discussion, negotiated with his son who agreed to pay the insurance after the first year. He was pleased, and his son was pleased. That seems like a successful outcome to me.

Sometimes prioritizing choices in a minimum, merely satisfactory, or most lavish framework alerts clients to their choices and lets them select a more appropriate option without feeling as if they have been deprived of something they really wanted. When clients grapple for a decision, it helps to make a chart of their choices for them. Note that the client will be more likely to buy into a decision in which he has been a participant.

Minimum, Merely Satisfactory, and Most Lavish Goals

	Item	Cost	Advantages	Disadvantages
Minimum:	Used Japanese car	$14,000	Low cost, low insurance	Undetermined reliability
Merely Satisfactory:	New American car	$25,000	Mid-priced insurance, new condition, good looking	None
Most Lavish:	SUV	$36,000	Good looking, traction	High upkeep, high cost

I run off a lot of quick charts to determine the best home purchase, retirement package, or car choice for my clients. Simple as they are, they get my clients thinking about what is important to them. I do not tell my clients which is the best choice for them but do begin a discussion of the merits of the various options. Guess what? When clients view their choices in black and white, they rarely choose their most lavish goal. They feel they can live without it, and pocket some money for other goals later on.

For many clients, the most lavish goal, which may be the one they came in with, is relegated to the wish list, and is rarely missed once the choice is made. First, I believe that many people are middle-of-the-roaders and instinctively take the middle choice that seems safer than the one on either end. I have seen this over and over again in retirement planning, when the client selects the moderate alternative just so they are not in the position of taking the one that pays them most now and leaves nothing to the spouse in the end, nor the one that pays the least now and leaves much to the spouse in the end. They say, "I will take the one in the middle." I wonder how many products are positioned this way, just to make a sale easier.

Second, clients often feel comfortable with a decision that provides them most of what they want without going out on a limb, rather than always having their first choice. Because people often feel undeserving of special rewards, they believe that having the most of what they want now will require some unforeseen sacrifice in the future, and they are reluctant to put themselves in that position.

4

Working with Clients

Family Problems

As an advisor who knows your clients' deepest secrets, you are almost part of the family, because you are privy to considerable personal information of the type usually not discussed outside the family circle. In addition to being chief confidant, you may be invited to weddings, dinners, and other family events. You feel compelled to attend funerals. But your role is "almost" family, because you are not a blood relative and do not share the self-interest of the family members. This is an advantage, because it puts you outside the family circle and allows you to maintain your objectivity.

You may witness numerous family occasions. I have attended my share of clients' life-cycle events, and have witnessed very private family moments. I have seen grown family members cry, have joined them in celebrations, and have been present when spouses belittled each other and children spoke abusively to their parents. After a while, family members generally seem to forget I am around or that I am not really one of their relatives, and act naturally around me. I try to do my job but stay outside family politics.

Two things I learned early on: Never criticize someone's relatives and never take sides. The person who complains about a spouse or child today may change direction and be their truest supporter tomorrow, but they will not forget unkind remarks made by a nonrelative. Do not align yourself on either side because you may be the person left without a chair when the music suddenly stops. In other words, the family members may resolve their differences and then realize that you are not one of them. Try to be friendly, join the family at their beach house if you like, dress down when appropriate, kid around with them, but keep your professional hat nearby at all times.

Sometimes, you might feel you just have to step into a crisis situation. For one mother-son pair, I had to define my responsibility as to whether I should report the 40-year-old son's aggressive behavior toward his frail 75-year-old mother to a city agency. I ended the war between the two generations by inviting a psychologist to attend a meeting at my office. Now, three years later, the mother still sees the psychologist. She has learned to stand up to her son and, as a result, the son is less of a bully.

Treading that Fine Line in Family Situations

When working with a family, you may notice that not every member is treated equally. No matter how the relatives relate to one another, it is very important that you treat each family member as an individual and as a respected part of the group. Start by learning all their names and positions in the family, even if they look alike as does a set of twins we know. Get to know their families, jobs, leisure times, and health situations so you can refer to these when you see them. A quick "How was your trip to Mexico?" or "Are you settled in your new vacation house?" goes a long way to showing you care enough to remember their personal lives and establishing rapport.

Recently, three siblings came to see me about their late mother's estate. The oldest sibling was an attorney who did not want to hear anyone else's opinion. The second sibling was a musician who was very outgoing and tried to dominate the conversation. The youngest sibling, the only woman, was a soft-spoken poet. She followed the conversation and tried to venture her opinions from time to time, but whenever she opened her mouth, her two siblings pounced on her with dismissive comments. I tried to invite her into the conversation at several points, but was not sure I was doing her a favor, exposing her to the brothers' anger. A day or two later, I called the poet to give her the chance to voice views she had not been able to bring up in my office.

If you are privy to personal information such as an illness or situation that requires particular financial steps, talk about the situation in clearly professional terms, work on the financial side, and do not mention it to other family members without the appropriate person's permission. When I see more than one family member, I always ask whether they would prefer to be in on the same meeting, or meet with me one at a time. Never assume that they share personal financial information with each other. You do not want to leak family secrets.

Should You Be the Negotiator?

I have often found myself in the position of negotiator for uncomfortable family situations and referee for all-out feuds. I have been in conference with family members who I thought just might do battle across my conference table; luckily, that has never happened. Most combative relatives rely on insults and pushing old buttons that they know will trigger an emotional response.

Many families have a gatekeeper who worries about the family's image and keeps the others in check. You will recognize the gatekeeper because that is the one who looks embarrassed during tense moments and says, "That is not what we came here for. This is not a therapy session." Generally, everyone feels guilty after that and things quiet down for a little while. This is your chance to regain control and focus the group on their finances.

If things get overheated, you have a perfect right to send clients home to argue in private. Give them a list of items you need to continue your work, such as common goals, spending habits, and estate planning desires. Tell them to return when they are beyond blaming each other and ready to reach a consensus. Shouting, "It's your fault!" may make one of the parties feel better, but it will not lead to financial problem resolution.

Mom and Pop as Advisors

Many financial planners are in small boutique firms, often with more than one family member. In the case of husband and wife, this can work to your advantage. Since you have experienced some of the same issues as your clients, such as buying the first home, educating kids, and caring for elderly parents, you can make an immediate connection. Clients feel they know you if you live in the same part of town or have kids at the same schools. They believe they can trust you because you are married. They think meeting your spouse helps them know you better.

However, you can play this to great advantage or run it into the ground. On the one hand, there could be a natural rapport between you and another married couple. My husband and I once met with a nice young couple who needed discipline in budgeting, paying down their debt, and saving for their future. They told us we would be their "financial mom and pop." Apparently, they wanted us to impose discipline on their financial lives. This spoke volumes about the homes they had been raised in and the carrot and stick that motivated them.

On the other hand, many people will not want to work with people who remind them more of their relatives than of professionals. Try to keep your professional distance. I truly believe that while a personal relationship can encourage prospects to feel comfortable initially, it can wear thin awfully fast. Not many clients want to feel like children with stern parents.

What happened to the young couple who wanted financial parents? After we did extensive financial planning for them and determined that they were dangerously in debt and living well beyond their means, they promised they would come back in six months to see if they were keeping within their budget and presumably to be scolded if they were not, but they never returned.

Getting Too Close: If You Are Too Much Like Them, They Will Not Come Back

It is natural to be attracted to clients you feel comfortable with and to shy away from people who make you uncomfortable. Many advisors complain about working with physicians, saying they are hard to get along with. I have never found them so.

Actually, physicians form about 45 percent of my practice. Why? Could it be because my brother and nephew are physicians, or a lot of my parents' friends were physicians? I like to work with doctors. I appreciate their intelligence, confidence in decision making, and dedication, but do not believe in a physician mystique.

On the other hand, you do not want to exhibit too much similarity to your clients' lives. Imagine going to a dentist, telling him your tooth aches, and he says, "Yes, I know how you feel. My tooth hurts me, too." Or going to a lawyer and you say, "It's such a nuisance filling out these forms," and she replies, "I have the same problem. I hate forms." You would probably be astonished. Clients do not want advisors to share too many of their concerns or confide too many of their own problems. They want advisors to be enough like them to be familiar with their situations, yet not close enough to fill their shoes.

Beware of Getting Too Close for Comfort

Do not tell your clients your personal problems.
Do not leak information about other clients.
Do not talk too much about your personal life.
Do not try to be their financial mom and pop.
Do remember clients are there to talk about their secrets, not about you.

I have had conversations with clients who live in my neighborhood, have children at the same schools my children attended, have a daughter who is an artist as mine is, vacation where I do, or use my hairdresser. I enjoy connecting to my clients, and do work with many people whose lifestyles are not so different from mine.

Sometimes, it is good to have a personal connection. Many clients will seek out a member of their social set (e.g., someone who belongs to their golf club or sits on the same charity boards) to do business with. Other times, although the rapport seems comfortable and you certainly have lots to talk about, you may be signing up a new dinner companion or golf buddy, but not a new client.

Why not a new client? Your similarities may be just a little too close for comfort. I believe some people think if you are like them, you will not know more than they do. Others worry that because you may have common acquaintances, some information about their finances may leak out inappropriately. Still others may just think they will not be comfortable running into you at social events once you know all about them. Finally, some clients want a guru to tell them the magic recipe for improving their financial lives, and if you prove to be an ordinary human being like they are, you cannot be their guru.

When you meet new clients, if the shoe fits too well, hold back. Now is not the best time for show-and-tell. When clients say they vacation every year at your favorite ski resort, no need to tell them immediately you go there, too. When they tell you their 10-year-old son is in the fifth grade at your child's school, no need to say your son is a seventh grader there just yet. Keep some personal revelations for later. Let your professional reserve keep you from spilling all the beans early in the relationship. It may be fun to compare notes in the first conversation, but if what you are looking for is a long-term client and not a new friend, keep the social chitchat to a minimum, and get down to business.

To determine how close you should get to your new clients, think about where they come from. If they choose you because you live on the same street or have children in the same school, it is all right to talk about your common interests for a short while at the beginning or end of the meeting. However, it is likely that if they got your name from the telephone directory or as a referral from another professional, they want an arm's-length relationship, and will not be happy to learn that you know many of the same people. Think about it—if they had wanted a referral to an advisor from the friends you have in common, they would have asked for one.

Do Not Impose Your Values

How can you, an expert advisor, know what is right for each client yet refrain from imposing your personal values on your clients? The first way is by listening. Hear what your clients want, how they would like to live their lives, and learn about the choices they have made. Then, just as you would for the various members of your family, allow your clients to live according to their own creeds.

One planner I know thinks all his clients would be happier if they were married. He often encourages his single clients to look for a significant other. His clients do not seem to mind and discuss their personal lives with him at length.

I do not believe imposing my values on clients is my role. Nor do I think one lifestyle would fit all my clients. Actually, one of the things that keeps my job so interesting is the many different ways people choose to live. Although he means well, I think that planner is crossing a line that makes me uncomfortable. My job description does not include matchmaking or proselytizing about marital unions.

To best serve your clients, hear your clients out, give them your professional advice, and respect their personal choices. Then you will have responded to what clients want most: to be heard, respected, and treated as unique individuals.

Lifestyle Choices

Which of the following is most true of your practice?

a. Most of my clients are like me.

b. Most of my clients are very similar to each other.

c. All my clients are very different from one another.

If your answer is (a) or (b), your day will undoubtedly be easier, but probably not very challenging. Once you have instructed one or two clients in what to do in their circumstances, will it really interest you to tell the same story to the next client?

Actually, it is unlikely that you will be able to find many clients who are very similar, even if they live in the same town or have the same career. One of the exciting parts of my practice is that every client is different and every situation is at least in part new. Sure, I have met people in debt and people who are wealthy. And

I have worked with widows whose husbands died much too soon (a specialty of mine) and young heirs to their grandparents' fortunes. But each situation is very different, each set of problems is new, and I would not have it any other way. I always learn a lot that I can add to my experience and knowledge with each new family. My suggestion is to value diversity in your clients as you do in investments.

If your answer to the previous question is (c), your time will be enriched. I say, "Vive la différence!"

But Is It Not Our Role to Say What We Think Is Right?

No matter how unusual the story a client relates, I try to be interested (which is usually not difficult), objective (it is their story after all), and most important, nonjudgmental (this is not a court of public opinion). I try never to apply my own values to their situations ("What! You are not married and plan to have a child?" or, "Your husband left you for not one but two younger women?!"). Rather, I put myself in the client's place and help work out solutions that best fit his problems.

I deal with the financial aspects of their problems. I do not question their lifestyle choices unless they are financially impractical. Even then, I point out the practical components of their decisions and lead them to see how their choices may impact their lifestyles in the future. I do not discuss the merits or disadvantages of a personal choice from any other standpoint. Very often, there is no right or wrong. There are so many possible lifestyle choices, that one size does not fit all.

I feel I am simply my clients' financial advisor, not their religious, moral, or ethical consultant. I have, however, dropped clients whose moral judgments led to irregularities that did not feel correct to me. I generally know very early in the relationship when I do not want to work with someone.

I have turned down clients who could not say where their money had come from, and others who were involved with organizations or activities that made me feel queasy. It was easy to turn away the man who wanted to hire me to invest millions of dollars that belonged to a cultlike organization he headed.

Unfortunately, there is no guidebook for what is right or wrong, but mature professionals can tell by their gut feelings what will not work for them. If a client's situation makes your stomach churn, your blood race, and puts your animal fight-or-flight response system on alert, listen to your body's cues and act accordingly.

Four Incredible Stories I Have Heard

1. *Married Is Better.* The planner I know who thinks people are happier married advised one never-before-married 70-something to abandon her picky ways and reconnect with the high school beau she had rediscovered. Instead of being insulted, this client brought her beau in for the planner's approval. Shortly after that meeting, a wedding invitation arrived in the mail. The happy couple will soon celebrate their first anniversary as husband and wife. Who says it is always wrong to give personal advice?

2. *Leave the Jerk.* Often, it is tempting to ask a client why he or she is in an unhappy and unfulfilling relationship. One of my clients, Jen, caught her husband giving her jewelry to his new girlfriend. Telling Jen to leave her husband may seem like good advice, but beware. If you tell a client to leave the jerk and they later reconnect, you may be the "jerk" who gets left. Jen and her husband reconciled, and I was glad I held my tongue. I suggest offering this advice only if the relationship seems to be abusive. Then you may take steps to legally protect the abused spouse.

3. *Matchmaking for Clients.* I have a client, Connie, who asks me at every opportunity if I can recommend a good stock and a good man. I do actually know some men she could meet and sometimes I think of her. Then I remind myself that I am not a matchmaker. If I give Connie's number to a man, and it does not work, will that be my fault? If they get along, but the man does not call back, am I responsible?

   I have gone as far as inviting two clients I think might like each other to the same educational roundtable in my office with other clients and letting nature take its course. If the match does not work, everyone's dignity is intact, and no one is to blame.

4. *Go Back to School and Change Careers.* Many of my clients decide to change careers just when they seem all set. One client recently

(Continued)

gave up a career as a successful prosecutor to pursue his dream of being an actor. Guess what? He is now appearing on a weekly television show.

I am happy to report I have encouraged clients to change careers, add to their education, and make a new start in life. And I have helped them decide the best ways to do so. I advised one newly divorced woman to train for a career so she would not be dependent on her former husband for the rest of her life. I have helped successful professionals leave their jobs and become the writer, carpenter, or sculptor they always wanted to be. If it works financially and fulfills them, I am glad to be a guiding force in this major change. Not part of the job description, you say? In this case, I feel working outside the box is justified by the positive changes in the client's life.

If It Goes against Their Grain, They Probably Will Not Listen Anyway, So Go Ahead and Tell Them What You Like

If you still feel you have something of value to add in the personal advice arena (dating, marriage, divorce, family, friends, child rearing), think about why you are doing it. One financial planner I met recently asks potential clients what church they attend. He wants to work only with people who share his religious faith. I consider that an inappropriate question. Church membership only becomes appropriate in a financial office if the clients are tithing part of their income to their church, and your clients will tell you that, anyway.

Do you need to be Dear Abby, or want supplicants to come to you like they did to the Godfather? Are you seeking power and gratitude or genuinely trying to help?

If your motives are pure, giving advice is not about your needs, and you think your advice is helpful, I suggest that you let it lie for 48 hours. On rethinking the situation, you may discover that the urge to dispense personal advice has subsided. If you want to go ahead, convey your personal advice gently. If your advice seems way out of character to your client, just like a person under hypnosis, your client will not act on it anyhow.

Gaining the Client's Confidence

There are many reasons you might want your clients to believe in you. First, you probably want them to be confident that they have chosen the right advisor, come to you with their problems, and be straightforward about their issues. Second, you want them to believe enough in your recommendations that they actually follow through, implement, and make use of your advice. If they have reservations, they might stash your plan in a drawer and take no action. Finally, clients who are confident in their advisors are more likely to refer their friends for advice. These referrals can be a great ongoing source of new business for you.

To achieve your clients' confidence, follow these four rules:

1. *One Hand.* Never tell your client that you are unsure about which way to go, because on the one hand option A has some advantages, while on the other hand, options B, C, and D have others. In presenting advice, it is best not to present too many hands. Explain your thinking clearly and the pros and cons of various actions, then—with your client—pick the option that most closely fits the need and keep to it.

2. *Leave Your Self-Doubt at Home.* If you are the kind of person who never is certain about anything, do not hem and haw. Tell your spouse and your siblings about your self-doubt, tell your office assistant if you must, but do not confess your inferiority complex to clients. How can they believe in you if you do not?

3. *Sooner Is Better.* If you delay seeing a client because you are busy and postpone appointments because something more pressing comes up, you will lose continuity and the client will sense something is wrong. He may attribute delays to a lack of care, incompetence, or inability to complete the work. Client appointments should be near sacred. Once interrupted, it becomes difficult to restore the client relationship.

4. *Do What You Say You Will Do.* (a.k.a.—do not change horses in midstream) After you and your clients discuss what needs to be done, follow through. Do not show up

with half a plan, leave out a promised section, or deliver a part of the expected outcome. Reliability is everything in an advisor.

Finding the Client's Comfort Level

Recently, I interviewed candidates for an administrative position at my firm. One woman, whom I liked very much, became very playful during her second interview. She teased a male colleague of mine, adding innuendo to every question. Her behavior was inappropriate in terms of professionalism and the natural evolution of a personal relationship. I doubt that we will offer her the position because this applicant made us feel uncomfortable, and we do not want to experience that again.

Most people want to feel comfortable. They want to be free to talk about themselves, find solutions to personal problems, and feel they have made a good choice in their advisor. Before teasing, shouting, bullying, or acting quirky, find your client's comfort level.

Sometimes, you will be surprised. I met two new clients, both very organized, detailed, neat, reserved, and proper in their behavior. When I introduced them to younger, more casual members of my staff, it amused me that they laughed long and hard at lighthearted remarks. Opposites really do attract. My staff drew them out of their shells, and that led to getting to know them better.

Yet, I would not startle anyone, use rude language, or do anything that might make a visitor to my office uncomfortable. I watch clients' reactions as we talk, and gauge how far we can go in conversing, joking, probing, and offering information about ourselves.

There will be telltale signs when you are approaching the edge of the comfort zone. These can include a hush in the conversation (this means you might have already gone too far), a sudden change in the topic (meaning stay away for now), a folding of the arms (do not go there), or a turning of the body away from you (which means the client does not want to deal with that now). Watch out for these danger signs:

Fidgeting

Folded arms

Turning of the body away from the speaker

Covering the face

Changing the topic

A sudden silence

All these attitudes are red flags. Something you have said or done has pushed the client outside the comfort zone. These actions are something you should listen to, or you will lose the client's confidence.

If you reach the danger zone, picture yourself driving a car. As the driver, you are in charge. Slow down, shift gears, change direction, take a detour, and think of new ways to reach your destination.

Frequently Recurring Client Fears and Glitches

Siblings: Unfinished Business

Sibling relationships can be very complex. I have met many siblings over age 60 who still wonder whom mother loved best. This insecure feeling can color their sibling relationships for life.

Sibling issues often show up when caring for elderly parents, distributing family assets, selecting advisors to handle family investments, and settling the family estate. Deep down your adult client may, at times of family stress, feel like a child who is being ignored and revert to old ways of dealing with family issues. Writing this has made me revisit my own family situation. When I was a child, the youngest of three, my older brother and sister would stay up late talking. When I tried to join in, they would say to each other, "Did you hear the wind? Must be a windy night outside." I was hurt, but took the hint and left them to their own conversation. I have not thought about that for many decades, and do not think I have been negatively affected by it. If anything, it encouraged me to speak up for what I believe in. However, think of the many people who have buried memories, real or imagined slights, and are still carrying around childhood hurts and poor relationships with siblings.

Recently, I met three siblings whose parents left them considerable assets, which they put in an account that they held as tenants-in-common. That meant any one of the siblings could withdraw money without the approval of the others. When the eldest son withdrew $125,000 to put a down payment on his new home without consulting his siblings, the roof fell in. Financially, it was as if each of his siblings had contributed $40,000 toward their brother's house. After several phone calls and one meeting in my office, we figured out a way for the oldest brother to repay the money with interest within five years, and everyone felt better.

If you have elderly clients, it is a good idea to head off problems by meeting with them and their children and explaining the family finances to all members who will be affected. When a problem arises down the road, you will know which siblings to call. At the same time, when the children meet you as the family advisor, they will know that they should call you and, presumably, continue to work with you after the death of the parents.

If you are faced with the sudden death of one of your clients and you have not yet met the children, try to schedule a meeting in your office a few days after the funeral while all the children are in town. Find out what each sibling's needs are, the terms of the estate, and who the other advisors are. Ask how you can be of help. Your conversation might include:

Planner: Have you decided who will handle your mother's estate?

Older Sibling: I am the executor of the will, so I will do the paperwork. I have already hired my mother's attorney to help me.

Younger Sibling: You know, mom was giving me $10,000 each year, and I am going to need that amount in the future.

Older Sibling: The will calls for equal distribution of assets. It does not mention anything about special gifts to my sister.

Planner: I have a copy of the will. I will go over it, call your attorney, and discuss the terms and any special distributions. Then I will call each of you to let you know what we have found. If the will does not provide for distributions, then it is not an estate issue. You [the youngest sibling] and I should sit down and decide what you really need and determine where to go from there.

Younger Sibling: Great! I do not want to worry that I will be left with nothing.

Older Sibling: Let me know if there is anything you need me to get for you.

In this conversation, you have put yourself into the situation without alienating anyone. What might have turned into an emotional confrontation between two siblings, now is a plan to gather information about the estate and explore the hard-pressed younger sibling's finances, and then move forward from there. You have defused a potentially hot situation.

Whatever you do, do not side with any one sibling. You should be neutral about family situations, and concern yourself with resolving financial issues. Maintain an arm's-length stance and deal with substantive issues in an objective way. Understand that

Ten Methods of Arriving at a Compromise

1. Hear everyone out.
2. Do not let any one person dominate the conversation.
3. Do not permit yelling or acting out at the meeting.
4. Do not dwell on old family issues.
5. Let each person have a chance to speak.
6. Do not take sides.
7. See what each person can live with.
8. Offer a compromise position.
9. Modify the position until objections diminish.
10. Set the plan in motion with a to-do list for all parties.

tempers may be short during this time of personal loss. While emotions swirl around you, your job is to be the voice of reason and calm. If you know the wishes of the deceased, you can explain and reinforce them. If the affairs of the estate are disorganized, you can bring organization to them. If there are no other advisors involved, you can make recommendations for the appropriate professional help that is needed.

When one of my clients, Carolyn, died suddenly, leaving an alcoholic husband who could not control his finances and two grown children who did not speak to each other, I took on the role of peacemaker for the family. My goal was to get things done and see that Carolyn's wishes, which she expressed clearly to me but not as clearly in her estate documents, were carried out. Whenever I was faced with irate family members in my office or on my phone, I reminded myself that I was taking care of family business for Carolyn. After two years, things are better for that family. Once they learned the parameters, including that the husband could not fritter away all the money that Carolyn intended for her four grandchildren, things calmed down.

Let all the family members have their say, keep the conversation professional and geared to getting things done, and minimize family conflicts. Be gentle at this delicate time, and you may have a new generation of clients for life.

Poor Little Rich Girl or Boy

Many of my clients grew up in well-to-do households. They have had advantages that money can buy including private educations, exotic vacations, and beautiful homes. These perks, however, often come at a high emotional cost.

One of my clients, Randall, has never worked. He has many millions in trust just for him, but he is afraid to spend much of it. Since he has no job-related income, and indeed has not been trained to work at anything, he worries that he will run out of money one day.

Randall has never had to make decisions or plan ahead and seems incapable of doing so. Nor did he receive much attention from his well-traveled parents. He does have a secret plan, though. If he runs out of money, which is very unlikely given his cautious style of living, he can move to a family vacation home on a lake in the Adirondacks. In Randall's case, financial excess has led to stunted financial responsibility.

For many young heirs, inexperienced but faced with financial responsibility, the money can be as much a burden as a joy. For some, the following equation holds true:

$$\frac{\text{A Great Deal of Money}}{\text{Too Little Responsibility}} = \text{Financial Immaturity}$$

Randall needs a safe place to develop his financial prowess. He can begin by handling small amounts of money, making personal decisions, meeting the advisors for the family trust, and doing volunteer work to develop skills and a sense of self-worth. If you have a Randall in your practice, it would be easy to let him become dependent on your advice and thereby remain a long-term client. Just like the parable about giving a hungry man a fish and providing him with one meal or teaching him to fish and allowing him to get his own food for life, it might be more satisfying to you and useful to him, however, to educate Randall and show him a way to become self-sufficient over time. Whatever you do, do not tell Randall he has so much money that he does not need an advisor or a financial plan. Randall is very needy and will feel rejected, frightened, and lost. Working with Randall can actually be great for your practice, because he knows many people who grew up as he did.

Randall's sister Molly may be daddy's (or granddaddy's) little girl, and may begin to resent that relationship with the powerful adult in her life. Molly may expect to be given the comforts in life. She likes to live well and spends as if her pot of gold is bottomless. You can help Molly by listening to her concerns and showing her how to step out of that role into adulthood.

One client of mine, Joanna, a 44-year-old writer, lives solely on her father's money. Her marriage broke up because her father didn't approve of the husband and she did not want to risk losing the monthly allowance daddy gives her. At the same time, she resents being beholden to her father and explaining her spending habits to him. I have counseled Joanna to tell her father she would like to have her own bank account and portfolio and not be so dependent on him. So far he is listening. I think Joanna's next step should be to approach her father with a well-thought-out plan for what she will need and how she will manage her funds. I think her father will respect a focused plan of action.

Whenever possible, I prefer to organize meetings with both generations, put all the sore points on the table (with my client's permission, of course), and discuss all the issues. Usually, when both members of the family learn each other's needs, feelings, and concerns, we can work out a compromise they both can live with.

Some Day My Prince Will Come (Not)

Many women walk into my office with a some-day-my-prince-will-come mentality. This is an outgrowth of the Cinderella story that American girls grow up reading and dreaming will happen to them. Some day, they are told, if they are extra good, a prince will come to save them from the hardships and disappointments of an unplanned and ordinary life.

You will know if your clients are Cinderellas by asking:

Have you prepared for your future?

How are you planning for retirement?

Are you planning to purchase a home?

Have you done estate planning?

If she has done nothing to prepare for the future, and her financial life is on hold—that is, she has a temporary job, temporary apartment, and no plans for changing her future—you may have a princess wanna-be in your office. If your female clients' lives seem temporary, or on hold, they may be adherents of this dream.

I am very sympathetic and understanding to women who hope for this scenario, and you should be, too. I grew up believing I would be saved from having to work, support myself, or plan for my retirement by a man who would take care of all that. Although I did marry (and am still married), at some point a light went on in my mind, and I realized I should be proactive in planning my own life. But many women I meet are not that far evolved (financially speaking).

Think of this as the good-woman syndrome: If you are a good woman, taking care of family, working, being responsible, moral, and loyal, someone will in turn take care of you. Unfortunately, this is not necessarily so. Explain this carefully to your female clients (they half suspect the truth, anyway) and offer yourself as a steady source of advice and planning for the future. While you will not be her white knight, and should not hold yourself out as one, perhaps you can fill a void in your client's life. Some women do prefer to transfer this fantasy to men, and therefore prefer male advisors of a particular age (depending on their own stage in life) to serve this mentor role for them. Others want to work only with a female advisor, who can, through her example of competency and professionalism, bring them back to reality.

Even very accomplished, successful, well-educated women often hope and even expect to have some help through their financial rough spots in life. I help my clients learn that the white-knight syndrome may not work for the following reasons:

- Women are marrying later. Just check the ages in the wedding announcements in your newspaper.

- Women are often widowed in their thirties, forties, fifties, or sixties and live way beyond the time their husbands died. The average widow's age at the husband's death is reported to be 56.

- Even women who are not widowed at young ages typically outlive their husbands by six or more years.

Fortunately, most women are open to hearing that they will need to take responsibility and compensate for a slow start in the financial area. If you can help your female clients educate themselves, you will keep them as loyal clients forever. What do women want in an advisor-client relationship? They want security, stability, and professionalism. They want to be taken seriously, to be given information, to be educated, and to be included in decision making. These are the keys to the kingdom of female clients.

Bag-Lady Syndrome

Women really do have special needs and concerns. I have had many female clients, including successful physicians, attorneys, and corporate executives, tell me that they fear ending up as a bag lady. In their worst nightmares, these women can actually picture themselves living on the streets, wearing tattered clothes, scrounging for food, and pushing bags of belongings around with them. No man has ever shared a similar fantasy with me.

Where does this fear come from? That is easy—it is the reverse of the good-woman syndrome. Women with this fear have read the same fairy tales, but have a more pessimistic outlook. What if her prince takes a wrong turn, and meets a princess the night before their supposed encounter? What then? These little girls grow up, get educated, have careers, but live in fear that things will turn sour, no one will want them or care for them, and they will descend to the dregs of society.

Do all women dread this scenario? Definitely not. But enough do so that you should be prepared to encounter it and talk your clients through it by setting up a financial life plan that they can achieve. That should drive out their fears and do away with bad dreams.

In contrast, most male clients I meet have more of a pick-yourself-up, dust-yourself-off, and start-all-over-again mentality. They think they might fail (and some of them do) and even lose everything (and some have done that, too), but they believe they will have another chance to make things right. In other words, they have learned to rely on themselves. Perhaps because their fantasies do not revolve around a significant other coming to save them from poverty and drudgery, but on their own ambitions, skills, and endless possibilities, along with a certain amount of bravado, they are more positive that a happy ending lies ahead.

I Will Hold On to This Stock Until It Gets Back to Where I Bought It

This strategy may have more to do with a client's ego than with investment planning. Few investors like to admit that they have picked losers. It is easier for a client to ignore a poor investment and hope some day it will get back to where it once was than to make necessary changes in his portfolio.

If you want your client to take action, point out the lost opportunity cost of holding on to deadwood rather than moving ahead with another choice that is more likely to perform well. Do not assign blame or mention who chose the investment. Deal with it objectively and present a solution that includes how to get the asset out of the account cleanly and simply.

Remember, for your client this is just as much about ego as about the asset. If the client refuses to budge, place the asset on a list of items that should be changed instead of singling it out; that will protect your client's ego from feeling further bruised.

If your client refuses to act, ask why this one asset matters so much. You can learn a lot from the answer. Some answers I have heard are:

"I like the company."

"I know someone who works there."

"My best friend told me to buy it."

"It was a gift from my Aunt Polly."

Do not counter with a report on the company, because that is not the issue here. Give your client suggestions for another company or sector of the market that is expected to do well, and start with a clean slate.

If all else fails, tell the client to take the decline in the asset as a tax loss to balance any capital gains for that year. Then you can turn lemons into lemonade.

But My Late Husband Chose This Investment

This comment has Danger: Emotional Zone written all over it. For some people who experience a sudden loss, keeping the portfolio the way it was formed by a loved one is similar to keeping grandma's ring. There is a very strong emotional tie to maintaining something that reminds the client of the loved one. Even though many wives have assumed responsibility for the finances in the home, I find this situation more common of my female clients than my male clients, so I will restrict this section to talking about widows.

Very often, when working with a widow, I encounter a portfolio that needs a complete spring-cleaning. When I explain this to the client, she may say, "My husband was a successful investor, and he chose all these investments." When I ask how long ago that was, the answer ranges from recently to as long as six or seven or even 10 years ago. I do not comment on the late husband's investment choices or performance. I do not criticize nor confront past decisions. I stick solely to what we can do going forward (see sidebar on facing page).

I carefully explain that since her husband died, we may have had two new presidents of the United States, been at war, raised or lowered interest rates, faced a bull (or bear) stock market, and experienced many other significant changes. I suggest her husband most likely would have reevaluated the portfolio many times, and probably would have made several changes by now. Typically, at that point the client loosens up and agrees to at least review and quite likely allow changes in the account.

I Will Be Really Happy When I Hit $10 Million

Most people have a secret success button that to them signals they have made it. For some, it is buying their own home, educating their kids, affording a fancier car, or a promotion. Sometimes the choice comes from unfulfilled childhood dreams, or remembering what their parents could not afford. For others, it is a magic number, and frequently a large one. My husband calls it the enough principle. That is, people feel secure when they have enough to reach their dreams. For all people, it is a target they dream of reaching. To know what the button is for each client, ask an open-ended question. Choose from among these, use a combination, or create your own:

When will you feel successful?

What is your ultimate goal?

How will you know when you have hit your target?

All three questions allow clients to express their desires in their own ways. That may not be in financial terms, nor even in very concrete ones. For example, some people may know they have hit their target when they own three homes, or when they have educated all their children. You may have to follow several paths to get their goals into financial language. One person's house may cost $100,000, while another's may be in the $2 mil-

Ten Steps to Revamping a Loved One's Portfolio

To loosen up a recalcitrant widow, try these techniques:

1. Ask about the person who created the portfolio, what he did in his career, about the marriage and family. It helps you learn about the family's background, and allows the widow to bring the situation into the open.
2. Talk about the deceased's investment style and success with investing. This will put you in the family's camp and give you an interesting history to work with. You may find that the widow knows more about what has been going on with her investments than even she thinks she does.
3. Try to get records of the portfolio to make your job simpler. This will help you determine what changes to make in the account.
4. Find out about other advisors to the family. This will give you information about the portfolio and other professionals to work with, so you will not be struggling in a vacuum. If it seems beneficial, ask if you can speak to these advisors about the account.
5. Ask the client for permission to review the account. This is a gentle start to the process of change.
6. Assure the client you will not make changes without her approval. This will give you time to assess the situation and your client's commitment to keeping things as is, and will brand you as a cautious, patient advisor.
7. Present your client with your findings. Invite other family advisors to the meeting to legitimize your work and make the client comfortable.
8. Allow enough time for discussion and questions about your recommendations. I usually allow two hours for each meeting. Educating the client will likely lead to understanding and accepting your recommendations and doing away with resistance to changes imposed by you, the expert.
9. Get the client's agreement to implement. She may want time to think it over and discuss the proposed changes with family members, and that is fine. If you push too hard, your client may retreat. If the account has not been touched in some time, two more weeks probably will not matter.

(Continued)

10. Report back frequently to the client as the changes take place. This is always a good strategy with a new client, and even more so with a concerned one. This can cement your relationship for the future.

This 10-step process will eliminate much of your client's initial reluctance and fear of change. You will lead the client slowly and carefully to the place you think she should be, and she will be more comfortable and feel more confident as she proceeds along this new path.

lion range. Further discussions will shed light on the details. First gather the criteria for someone's target; you can always do the number crunching later.

When clients tell you what they think, press them to elaborate on their secret goals. Ask why a certain accomplishment or number will satisfy them. As their financial advisor, you are in the prime position to determine how realistic their goals are.

My client Michael had $2.3 million when we first met. His wealth came from shares in his family's business. Michael lived very simply, and at age 37 was contemplating marriage and the purchase of his first house. He seemed to have every material thing he needed. Michael confided that he would be happy when his assets reached $10 million. That was the magic number that encapsulated Michael's desire for security and success. Michael did not plan to need or spend that money, just to leave it to his as-yet-unborn children, as his parents had bequeathed money to him.

Sometimes, when I teach, I tell my students about Michael and his target. They never fail to feel anger toward him because he is dissatisfied even though he likely has more money than they will ever have. They consider him greedy and undeserving of such wealth. They do not consider Michael's privileged background or his emotional needs. I explain that goals are good at any level of wealth. Michael should not be faulted for having lofty goals; in his social circle, those goals are not extraordinary. His goals will help him plan for his future and motivate him to work and save. If reaching for $10 million makes your client save, invest, and plan for his future, why is that wrong? I think it is not.

I show my students how Michael's attitude can help them think about their own goals. Michael's goals are not unrealistic. At his parents' deaths in the decades to come, he will inherit several million more dollars. With his continuing work in the family business, wise investment choices, and a long time horizon, Michael might well achieve his goals—as my students can achieve theirs.

Once you know your client's secret wishes, you become privy to very personal information. Use it to work closely with your client. Now you are in a position to help the client get on the right track. Go with your client's wishes and see how near to fruition they can come.

I Am Nervous. The Stock Market Is Going Down. I Want to Sell.

Some clients panic at each fluctuation in the stock market. To them skies look blue when stocks are up. They think stocks will continue to rise forever, and may be happy to buy at high levels.

However, when stocks decline, clients may want to bail out before the market hits ground zero. Such panic shows feelings of insecurity, fears about ending up in the poorhouse, and general impatience. This can be a real test of the bond you have with your clients, their respect for you, and your communication skills. If you have been communicating well with your clients all along, you are much less likely to receive panic calls during times of market uncertainty. To paraphrase an old saying, "Train your clients well in the ways you wish them to grow, and they shall be yours forever." While they may not have confidence in the markets at a particular time, they will have confidence in you and your ability to decide what is best for them.

Recently, I spent three hours in my office with a client who could not get past the what-ifs. "What if my mutual funds all lose money at the same time?" she asked. "What if my income is not enough?" "What if I run out of money?" I was ready to give up, because the explanations that sounded good to me, did not alleviate her concerns. Then I checked myself. I was reacting in a practical way with historical data. That was not what she wanted to hear. She was seeking emotional support and wanted me to listen to her fears and then present the confident "You will be fine" comment that I really believed.

Speak to your clients' fears as well as to the realities of the market, and you may well keep them calm and focused on long-term goals. Simply showing stock market charts to this client will not work because information cannot alleviate emotional fear. To reach these clients, teach them from the outset about investing and reaching their goals. In troubled times, assure them the sky is not falling, and that you are there to monitor the portfolio.

If you have a client who is fearful no matter what you say or do, you will have to decide how much time to give. This may not be a relationship you want to pursue. In my own practice, however, I have found over time that clients who run scared when they read the morning news *can* learn to trust my judgment and relax about their account if I directly discuss their concerns. Most of my skittish clients are glad to have their worst fears addressed and feel more confident thereafter.

Instead of being afraid to discuss their fears, ask clients what they think might happen in a worst-case scenario. Ask if they have ever experienced serious loss. Find out what is causing them to react to uncertainty so severely.

How to Respond to a Nervous Client

1. *Address the Emotional Issues First.* Very nervous clients will probably not absorb new information until they feel more relaxed and comfortable.
2. *Educate Your Client.* Think of simple information as the keys to true understanding. When your client understands how things work and what the goals are, it will be easier to stay calm.
3. *Call Clients Before They Call You.* You know who is most likely to call you after an active day in the markets or an unfavorable article in the paper. Stave off their anxiety by beating them to the phone call. This can cement your relationship and make you the good guy or gal on the block.

I Coulda, Woulda, Shoulda

If your clients are like mine, they constantly berate themselves. They could have bought Snapple when it was low, they should have invested their money in that technology company that earned 200 percent in one year, and they would have bought themselves a bigger house 10 years ago if they had only known that real estate would do so well over the last few years. Finance is one area in which people frequently think poorly of themselves. I have heard so many clients tell me how stupid they are and how little they know.

Everyone knows now what they should have done, but they forget how it was not all so clear at that time. They also do not admit that they might not have wanted to take the risk. For example, one of my clients, Hilda, told me that she wished she had invested in the same companies her son did and earned the same return. I reminded her that she was very conservative, feared losing money, and wanted 50 percent of her portfolio in bonds. She agreed that she did not want to take the risk associated with the greater returns. But I know we will discuss this again and again. She will see her son's winners, ignore his losers and the fact that at the time she did not know for sure which companies would perform well.

People in the shoulda fraternity lack self-confidence about their personal choices. Maybe they were constantly criticized by parents or teachers when they were children, or are now criticized by spouses or bosses. Some suffer self-doubt because of feelings of inferiority.

Try to cure your clients' wishful thinking about the past. Tell them not to beat themselves up over lost opportunities, and to go forward from where they are today. Give them your permission (which is probably what they most want—someone they respect to approve their choices) to take lower risks, to be who they are, and to forget about the past. Point out that they are more likely to reach their current goals by looking forward, not back.

Tell them to rank themselves on a scale of 1 (lowest) to 10 (highest) for each item on the following Self-Competency chart:

I am happy with who I am.

I am uncomfortable taking great risk.

I do not want to think about what might have been.

I am happy looking at the future.

I am comfortable living the way I do.

I do not like to worry.

I do not like uncertainty.

I know that I am different from my neighbors, friends, and colleagues.

I am pursuing a path that is right for me.

I make decisions that suit me most of the time.

If your clients score at least 60 out of a possible 100 on this chart, they are on the road to self-realization, and that is good enough. If their score is below 50, you have a permanent second-guesser on your hands. Prepare to do a lot of reassuring as your relationship continues.

Please Do Not Tell My Wife

It seems once or twice each year I encounter the don't-tell-on-me syndrome. My client Harold was in this situation. He had been married to Dora for over 20 years, and they had planned to grow old and live comfortably together. As they got older, and Harold neared retirement, he decided to speed up their accumulation of money by investing in some highflyers that his friends recommended. Harold lost almost all his savings, just as his wife was getting ready to move into the retirement mode.

Harold came into my office all excited. He had this problem, he said, and maybe I could help him. He poured out the whole sad story of botched investments and depleted accounts. Then he ended with a plea, "Please do not tell my wife what I have done."

I told Harold that I could try to help him rebuild his retirement account, but on three conditions. First, he would have to continue working and saving well past his planned retirement date. Second, he would have to listen to me about what to spend, how much to save, and where to put his money. Third, we would have to come clean about the whole situation with Dora. Harold agreed reluctantly. I think he felt guilty enough to try to right his wrongs. Actually, he had that resigned look of a mouse caught in a trap.

When he came back with Dora, he very nervously confessed what he had done. Dora, however, took it all very well. Apparently, she had experienced other similar lapses during her life with Harold. She immediately got to the crux of the matter and offered to be the keeper of the family checkbook and savings account. Dora became an ally in the fight against poverty.

I met with Harold and Dora on a regular basis for several years. Harold had one more setback when he made one more secret, foolish investment decision. I guess you cannot wholly change someone's stripes. This couple should soon make it to retirement, a little late, and perhaps not quite at the level they hoped to reach initially, but comfortable nonetheless. Now if we could only tie up the money so that Harold cannot access it at all, they would really be home free.

The moral is, do not buy into your client's childish fantasy that no one will know he is the guilty party. These may be the same people who, as children, told their teacher that the dog ate their homework and really thought she believed them. They think they can fool people, and the careless stuff they did will somehow go away.

As a professional, you should not allow your clients to keep secrets from their spouses or partners, and you should not be party to deceit and duplicity, not even if the situation seems relatively benign. No matter how clients press you, tell them cloak-and-dagger intrigue is not part of your job description and avoid impending disaster. Participating in such a deception is a sure way to lose clients for life.

CHAPTER

6

Being Available

How Much of You Do Clients Get?

Financial planning is a very personal business, and you are the one your clients want to be personal with. Just like students in a classroom, they all want to know that they are special and important to you, that you like them and approve of their lifestyles, and that they can count on you being available to them whenever they feel they need you.

I do not mind letting clients lean on me for emotional support or helping them establish their goals or even helping them iron out some family problems. I have always been a people person, and enjoy meeting clients and sharing a small part of their lives.

I have learned that this business means being available to my clients in their moments of need or uncertainty. I have received a phone call from a client shopping in a carpet store inquiring about the affordability of a particular rug. I have had calls from clients at brokerage offices asking which investment to pick and bank managers' offices wanting to know which mortgage to choose.

A Cry for Help

Client: I am here at my bank asking about a mortgage. The branch manager has offered me two kinds of mortgages and I do not know which to take.

Planner: What are the terms of the two mortgages?

Client: One has points, and the other does not.

Planner: What are the interest rates and the length of each mortgage?

Client: I do not remember. What should I do?

Planner: Is the manager there now? Can I speak to him?

In this conversation, the planner listens and notes that she has to take charge. After the bank manager explained the choices clearly, the right one for this client became apparent. In other cases, further research may have to be done. Most important, convey to your client that you want to help with their difficult choices. This is an opportunity for you to provide value-added to your client for a little extra time and effort. Your client will remember your availability and willingness to help and in most cases will reward you with long-term loyalty.

What would have happened if I had not been at my desk when those calls for help came through? Would the clients have survived and made their own decisions or delayed those decisions for a later time? Probably yes. They might have asked someone else, delayed, or otherwise managed to get through the moment. However, all these clients expected and preferred that I be available to them precisely when it benefited them most.

These clients are not so different from my general client population. I remember one vacation in Disney World, Florida, with my husband and two young children, waiting in line for lunch while my husband hustled to the phone banks (in the days prior to cell phones) and returned an anxious client's call as her stocks tumbled for the day. That one call disturbed the peace of our long-awaited family vacation, but we chose to make the call and comfort the client. Of course, you have choices and can decide each instance based on its importance.

I do feel I am entitled to a private family life and should not constantly be at the beck and call of my clients. The question is where to draw the line while observing your commitment and satisfying client needs. First, there must be a line, or your clients might ring your doorbell on Sunday morning as you emerge from the shower. Second, if you do not set a line, you will soon burn out. Third, your usefulness to your clients will diminish in proportion to the amount of time you spend in your office when you should be relaxing elsewhere. And just between you and me, most crises can wait until after the weekend, anyway.

Think about setting limits that nothing short of a 1929 stock market crash can breach. In the last few years, I have decided that in the summer months I will leave work on Thursday night and spend a three-day weekend at my country house. So far, I have been very successful. Almost nothing interferes with my Thursday-night rule. My staff has my phone number, and some calls from my office do come through on Friday. However, as I head out the door on Thursday nights, sometimes with my portable computer, I know I am moving in the right direction.

Making the Relationship Personal

I enjoy being invited to clients' family gatherings, and I go whenever I can. I like seeing how my clients live, sharing tales of precious photos or souvenirs, and meeting their friends and families. In other words, I find it fun and helpful to our relationship if I see clients in their native habitats once in a while. But what do you do when each invitation you accept leads to two more? Instead of performing a duty to your clients, you may find your duty never ending.

One of my clients, Carrie, invited me to a concert in her home. Her sister, she said, played the violin, and they were inviting some friends to an informal concert. My attendance to the concert seemed so important to Carrie that I gritted my teeth and prepared for an unexceptional performance. Much to my surprise, Carrie's sister played beautifully. Her biography listed performances at Carnegie Hall as well as many others around the globe. I had a wonderful time, met friends and family, and enjoyed delicious homemade food as well. I felt lucky to be there. The only downside has been that now the family invites me to every performance, and I cannot always go. I do make sure to let them know how disappointed I am to miss such a lovely evening.

Recently, I happily attended the wedding of another client, Vera, who had waited decades to be reunited with her first sweetheart. What a wonderful ceremony and reception it was! Relatives had come from all over the country to join in the celebration. The bride was radiant, and the groom was resplendent in his ceremonial kilt. I would not have missed Vera's special event, and indeed did pass up a weekend in the country to be there.

Another client, Roseann, asked me to a string quartet recital in a senior citizens' residence. Although I am fond of Roseann, the 90-minute drive each way, the rainy weather, and what was likely to be a very long evening dissuaded me from accepting the invitation. I declined and sent Roseann a note congratulating her on her musical accomplishment.

When deciding how much socializing is appropriate, think about the social customs where you live. In some big cities, where anonymity reigns, it might be unusual to socialize with your clients more than just occasionally, although one accountant I know in New York City told me she built her whole business on contacts made at the local chamber of commerce. In smaller cities, business is often conducted in a social setting: over dinner, at a club, or on the golf course. If that is true in your town, you might want to practice your golf swing.

One colleague of mine lives in a town of 6,000 people. He says his clients are people he socializes with regularly. When the editor of a local paper wants a financial column, she turns to my friend. When the local men's club needs a financial speaker, they call you-know-who. My friend tells me his business networking is all done very informally. When I asked how he gets new business since he knows most of the people in his town, my colleague said there are just enough new people passing through to bring in some new business for him every year. Wherever you live, and whatever the culture, let the style of your community be your guide for just how much socializing you do.

If there is no social code in your town that determines how you should act, decide each case on its merits. Whether you accept or refuse, always keep the door open for the next time. Sometimes you will want to go, other times it may be professionally wise to attend in order to meet the next generation of clients or friends who can become your clients, and still other times you may choose to stay away. When you have a conflict or your personal life is calling, think to yourself that you have done enough and then decline the invitation politely.

Deciding When Too Much Is Enough

If you feel that you are on call above and beyond the duty of a financial professional, instead of complaining to your spouse or commiserating with your colleagues, tell the client. How much is too much?

- If you are called at home during dinnertime . . .
- If you are expected at the office on weekends to meet a particular client . . .
- If you are asked to visit the client in her office or home instead of yours without good cause . . .
- If every time you think a job is complete, there is just one more thing . . .
- If the client demands to be put through to you right away every time he calls no matter what you are doing at that time . . .
- If the client demands immediate turnaround on every request . . .
- If you are called on at the last minute to drop all else . . .
- If any of the previous hold true, and it happens more than once or twice, it is time to lay the law down to your client.

At my firm, I am often willing to take extra steps to ensure that my clients are comfortable, following my advice, implementing my plans, and meeting with other professionals when necessary. My staff members have recently walked clients to discount brokerage offices to help them implement my investment recommendations, have accompanied them to attorneys' offices to see that they implement my estate planning suggestions, invited insurance agents to my office to meet the clients and discuss various policies, and coordinated telephone conference calls with my clients and their other advisors. Where I draw the line is a matter of the client's needs and attitudes, my sense of responsibility to that client, and what seems appropriate.

If a client who needs help is reasonable and values my assistance, I will be there. My staff members have even helped clients locate important information after the death of a loved one. But I have stopped short at cleaning out decades of files in basements and dens, because that is beyond reasonable. In one particular instance, I did arrange for the client to meet a responsible college student who was willing to do the work, but the client did not want to pay her a reasonable hourly fee and so did not hire her.

Basically, I think your practice will benefit if you take the extra step and do the nice thing for your client. Good deeds may well be rewarded down the road. However, I believe that you should protect yourself from clients who never know when their demands are too much. For me, too much is when you feel that someone is taking advantage of your time, your expertise, and your good nature.

Trust your instincts to signal when you have gone beyond the typical professional-client relationship. When you are asked to help with things that are not part of a financial advisor's job description, do not hesitate; tell the client that is not what you do. If you still have doubts, think about how other professionals respond. Does your lawyer, accountant, or dentist meet with you on a Sunday, come to your home, or respond to your personal needs in other unusual ways? If your clients are demanding much more of you, check with your colleagues or listen to your inner voice. Go that extra step for your clients, sympathize with their needs, help them find the right person for each concern they have, then set reasonable limits that work for you and stick to them.

Returning Calls within Twenty-Four Hours

One type of service that I am inclined to deliver to my clients and have my whole staff deliver as well is 24-hour turnaround telephone response time. When clients call, you should be able to get back to them by the next day even if it is just to check in, see what the call is about, and schedule a fuller conversation in the future if the question cannot be answered immediately.

Returning calls promptly is both polite and good business practice. I believe that telephone interaction represents all the emotional and personal aspects of the financial planning relationship: courtesy, respect, communication, listening, understanding, teaching, and judgment. Professionally, the call symbolizes the essence of information gathering and problem solving. To your clients, the rapidity of your response represents their importance to you and the dignity you bestow on them.

Is it enough to leave a message on your client's answering machine within 24 hours? I think so. It shows that you were responsive and tried to reach them. You are not responsible for no one being at home when you called. However, in most cases you should follow up again a day or so later. If there is simply no way you can get back to your client—for example, if you are away or speaking at a seminar—have someone in your office call and establish a time for your next conversation.

Returning calls promptly is important, because people can be hurt or annoyed when they feel ignored, disrespected, and not taken seriously. If you do this to a client more than once, it is hard to convince the client that you do care about her problems. It is imperative to call clients back before they call you a second time. Since you do not know when that will be, use my 24-hour rule. Always return calls within 24 hours, and your clients are likely to remain loyal to you.

E-Mail Protocol

I find that many people have dropped their manners when it comes to e-mail. Because it is fast and there is no client sitting across from you, it is easy to dispense with "Dear," "Thank you," "Sincerely," "Regards," and other niceties. To make a hit with your clients, take a minute to reestablish civility.

Always use your client's name, address the problem, and sign off with an appropriate ending. After all, even though at times it seems you are addressing a machine, there is a person reading your missive.

Unfortunately, due to the speed of the Internet, your e-mails have to be responded to quickly, just like telephone calls. On the other hand, you do not have to drop everything you are doing to sift through this mail. Check your e-mail once or twice a day and remember the 24-hour rule. If you are going to be away and do not plan to check messages, have someone else check your e-mail and notify clients when they can expect your response.

Finally, for your own records and for the sake of clarity, print out a copy of each query and your response, and put it in your client's file.

Ending a Meeting on Time While Showing You Care

I used to operate with time limits of one hour for prospect meetings and two hours for client meetings. That should keep things moving along in my office, right? Wrong. Unfortunately, people are not always predictable, and things do not always flow smoothly. This rigid guideline for meetings does not allow for differing personalities, human needs, individual styles, and varying degrees of interaction. Some people like to talk longer, others want to warm up with some small talk before getting down to the reasons for their visit, and still others want a slow-paced and relaxed meeting.

Differentiate between your clients and your prospects. For most prospects, 60 to 75 minutes should be enough. I tell prospects how much of my time they will have when we arrange the date of the meeting. I think anything beyond that tires out the prospect, causes the planner to lose focus, and puts a strain on a new relationship.

For existing clients, be careful to pay attention to their learning and listening styles. If you try to convey everything rapid-fire bullet style, you may not reach people who want things spelled out carefully. If you skip over one client's questions to observe your deadline for the meeting, you may confuse your client. Notice whether your client is absorbing the information, and proceed accordingly, slowing down or speeding up when appropriate.

Occasionally, I have people in my office who say what they have to say, give us materials they have compiled, ask their questions, and are gone within 15 minutes. These people are very rare. I think I see just two or three a year.

At the other extreme, I have clients like Albert, who comes to my office three or four times a year and likes to sit. He asks all his questions, expects greatly detailed answers, and looks wounded whenever I try to end the appointment. I usually tell Albert how much time I can spend with him when I make the date. That way, he knows what the parameters are. Albert always tries to squeeze in three more questions, even after I stand up and shake his hand good-bye.

Most clients fit somewhere between these two extremes. Some come with a list of questions and topics for discussion, a practice I encourage because it provides an outline for our meeting. Others think of their concerns as the conversation progresses.

My clients can have almost as much of my time as they want. My meetings generally run anywhere from one to two hours. Even when I am tight on time and everyone wants to come in the same week, I always schedule two hours between client appointments.

If you are having trouble getting clients to leave on time, try setting limits in advance. Tell your clients what you will be discussing and how long it should take. For clients like Albert who do not want to leave, send them an agenda before the meeting, and try to keep to it. I believe you can train your clients to respect your rules; doing so will bring order to the relationship, but you have to buy into this system yourself. Do not allow clients to break your rules with new questions just as you are getting ready to adjourn the meeting, much like the child who wants a glass of water to postpone bedtime just as you are about to turn off the light.

Learn to say, "We have covered a lot today. Let me think about these new issues and get back to you." To show you care, assure clients who do not want to leave that you will be thinking about their concerns. Then dash off a note within a week giving them some information that pertains to their case, even a brief thought, a solution to a problem, a suggestion of another meeting, or an article on the same topic. Knowing you care matters a lot to the Alberts of the world.

A Note to Albert

Dear Albert,

I was thinking about the gift you want to give your niece, and decided there are three ways you can go. First, you can give her a gift of up to $10,000 in cash each year. Second, you can put some money directly into her college education fund. Third, you might want to consider gifting some of your greatly appreciated stock to her.

I am enclosing an article that you might find of interest outlining the benefits of gifting stock.

Let us speak on the phone next week about advantages and disadvantages of each method, and the best way to handle this gift.

Sincerely,

This brief letter took very little time to compose, but will go a long way to making Albert feel cared for and valued. It helps solve one of Albert's most recent concerns and, at the same time, says I care about him, his problems, and his family. I suspect Albert will be very satisfied with my service.

Making House Calls

We know that most physicians stopped making house calls more than a generation ago. Now if you want medical service, you have to visit a doctor's office, a clinic, or a hospital. You must make an appointment in advance and be prepared to articulate your concerns. Almost no one expects a doctor to make home visits anymore.

However, I get many calls from clients and prospects who think it would be wonderful if I could visit them. Some are demanding people who insist on having their own way; others have good reasons for wanting home visits. I have made house calls to see clients who are elderly and disabled. I have even flown across the country to spend time with a client who is wheelchair-bound for life.

Nevertheless, I have refused to see clients who were not serious and seemed to be just amusing themselves by having different people entertain them with their skills, services, and products.

Sometimes the whole idea of home visits makes me feel less like a professional and more like a door-to-door brush salesperson.

If I know a client is serious about particular financial needs yet is immobilized by poor health or other circumstances, I will consider a home visit. My decision depends on need, what I can accomplish, my schedule, and the distance involved. I am more likely to go on a home visit if it is two hours or less by car than if it means being away from my home overnight. In that case, if the need is great, I will try to tie my visit to something else I must do in that city either personally or professionally.

I truly feel I can accomplish less out of my office where I have everything I need. I have to weigh and measure whether I am delivering quality advice in a professional manner when I am on a house call, or whether my client is getting an inferior service. If the latter is true, then I do not want to shortchange the client and will not travel.

In addition, I have the feeling that my work is devalued, that is, perceived as less valuable by clients, when I go running around out of my office. I think some clients grade your work less highly, and think of you as less professional, if you can be coaxed out of your office too easily. I have experienced the feeling that clients who talk you into their homes or offices do not think your work is worth as much. Think carefully before you agree to travel to see your clients. Sometimes it makes sense if you have several clients in another city and can set up appointments with many of them in one trip. Even then, I would consider renting a hotel suite or temporary office and inviting clients to meet me there or on other neutral territory, rather than in their homes. Then you can be the one in charge of the meeting—setting the time, place, duration, and agenda—and not be interrupted by phone calls from your client's next door neighbor or a dog who needs to be walked. "Have financial plan—will travel" does not generally work for me.

Recently, I was asked by a colleague if I would visit a $7 million man who wanted to meet me but disliked coming into New York City. The colleague assured me that this prospect was serious, but absolutely would not leave his home. I replied that if my colleague thought there was truly a great need, and that this would be a serious consultation, then I would entertain the idea. He is trying to set up the meeting now.

Another prospect, an elderly man, told me he wanted to meet me but he does not like taxis, buses, or subways. I declined to go to his house, but arranged for a private car service to bring him to my office from his home. At the last minute, he cancelled. I do not think we will ever meet, and that is okay. A serious prospect should be interested enough to meet you halfway, or you are unlikely to form the basis for a solid working relationship.

One of my new clients, Monroe, who has a bad temper, demanded that I come to his office to present my analysis of his portfolio, even though my agreement (which he signed) states that all work will be presented in my office. Monroe sounded like an angry child as he yelled over the phone that he would not come to my office and I must come to his. After discussing it with my staff, we agreed that the best solution would be to send a senior staff member familiar with Monroe's work to his office to present our findings. When we called to tell Monroe our decision, he made an appointment to come to our offices. Just like a spoiled child, he wanted his way, and once he got it, he did not want it anymore.

I feel better-prepared doing my clients' work in my office. That is truly where I have all my resources and am in my work mode. When I travel, I feel that I am in a vacation mode. It benefits my clients to come to my office. When I explain that, the great majority of clients understand. They probably feel the same about their workplaces. Judge each request on its own merits. Do not respond to client tantrums by packing your papers and travelling whenever you are called. Think about it: Are those the clients you want for life?

You Are Entitled to a Personal Life

Several years ago, my teenage son was at home alone when the phone rang. He answered, and was asked where his mother was. When he replied that I would not be home until later that evening, he received a barrage of anger from a client who decided she had to speak to me then. She was angry that I was not at home on a weeknight.

Hearing about that call was a rude awakening for me. I felt that I had to protect my private life and my family. I put a message on my answering machine that says, "You have reached ————. If this is a business matter for Karen or Lewis Altfest, they can be reached at xxx-xxxx during the hours of 9:00 to 6:00. If this is a personal call for a member of the family, please leave your message after the beep. Thanks for calling." My recorded message makes it quite clear that our home phone is for personal messages only. However, some people have bad manners, and there may be nothing you can do to prevent that entirely.

I still occasionally get business calls on my home phone. One morning, I was at home a little later than usual when Harriet, a widow, called to ask my help. We had never met, but Harriet had read about me in the newspaper and wanted to become a client. I asked Harriet to call my assistant at my office; she did and has been a client for years since. I am glad I was home that morning to answer her call. These calls come just often enough that I want my home phone number to be listed in our directory.

Actually, I believe although some of my clients seem to want me tied to my desk chair, most of them respect that I have an interesting and busy personal life. When I announce that I will be away for a few days or a few weeks—and I do so as much in advance as possible—they may seem taken aback, but then I find they are interested in my comings and goings.

I think their initial fear is similar to the August syndrome that many patients of psychiatrists and psychologists experience. They worry how they will survive their therapist's month-long absence, yet inevitably they do. Few situations are so pressing that they cannot wait a few weeks. For extreme emergencies, consider trading off with another planner and covering for each other, just as medical professionals do.

Do not change your plans to please one client. I have tried that, not around vacation dates, but around luncheon plans or theater tickets. Inevitably, the particular client who is having a problem resolves the issue or cancels the appointment. For clients who are so sensitive to crises that they zoom into an emergency mode, something that was so extremely pressing can apparently disappear as easily as it arose.

For the majority of your clients, having to rely on their own resources or delay getting professional input may actually be good for them. At the very least, it helps them analyze the problem so when they do get to you they are clear about their concerns. Furthermore, a modest wait can help your clients value the services you offer the rest of the time.

CHAPTER

7

Presenting the Plan

Finding the Right Time and Place

After I have analyzed my client's situation and come up with specific recommendations for action, I like to present my findings in a face-to-face meeting at my office. In-person meetings have many advantages, including allowing me to monitor my client's attitude and understanding, and strengthening my working relationship with the person sitting across the table.

I provide a comfortable, professional setting, just as I do for my prospect interviews, but I believe that any clean room with comfortable chairs and a hard surface, such as a desk or table, for your papers will suffice. I prefer to concentrate my energies on the intangibles of arranging a successful meeting: time, mood, and focus. It is important to select a time when I will not be interrupted as well as a time my client is not looking at her watch and wondering if she will be late for dinner. The mood should be serious but upbeat. Your client's financial life is a serious topic, yet there are generally positive approaches to financial problems, so there is no need to be too somber. Everyone at the meeting should be focused on the task at hand with few or no distractions. I usually call clients a week or two before I want to see them, so that we can pick the optimal meeting time. Then I box out that time on my calendar, so nothing else can interfere. I allow two hours per plan presentation, and usually allow another half hour to let me catch my breath before seeing the next client. I also like to have a safety cushion should my client's questions run over the scheduled two hours.

When clients come from out of town for the presentation, I set aside three hours' meeting time and order lunch or snacks. Experience has taught me that people who travel a considerable distance to my office and cannot return easily want all their questions answered before they leave. But I never schedule more than three hours because I find that people get foggy. Their minds become cluttered with too many details and cannot take in new information beyond the three-hour limit.

Surprisingly, if a client brings another professional (i.e., an attorney or accountant) to the meeting, the atmosphere will be even more focused and the time spent in small talk shorter. No one wants to seem like a dawdler. We all have our professional hats on from start to finish. Those meetings are usually completed in 90 minutes, and everyone moves on to the next appointment.

I never want my clients to feel rushed, and I do not want them to feel they only have part of my attention. There are very few emergencies that can interrupt my presentations: fire (but not our building's quarterly fire drill), serious family crises (but not minor problems that can wait), and urgent client or colleague situations (but not run-of-the-mill questions). Typically, about 1 in 10 of my presentations is interrupted, and then typically for less than three minutes.

The meeting is my time to turn my attention fully to my client, and my client's time to pay attention fully to the financial situation. Setting certain ground rules—such as letting the client know the length of the meeting in advance and providing a place for cell phones and young children to be left outside (I have even arranged for my staff members to entertain my clients' young children with computer games and videotapes)—heighten the meeting experience and deepen the advisor-client bond.

The three ingredients of a successful plan presentation setting are:

1. *Calm.* Peace, quiet, and a comfortable environment are key to attaining the ability to focus with the required intensity. This is the mood aspect of your office's stage set that is discussed in Chapter 2, an atmosphere of quiet, respect, and professionalism exuding from your office, your staff, and yourself.

2. *Concentration.* Once the client focuses on the material at hand, I do not want anything to break the thought process. It is too difficult to return to that level of attention. If construction workers are drilling outside your office, change your meeting place. If you have a heat, air, or noise problem, move elsewhere.

   For several months, there was a picture framer working on the floor above mine. His machinery made a loud banging noise and sometimes rattled the ceiling. There was no way to prepare for this interruption. I confronted the framer, and he denied making noise. I investigated rent regulations for office buildings in my area and found that his type of business was not appropriate above street level in our building. Before I could decide what action to take, he had packed up and moved.

   Although your plan presentation is not an exam, the tenseness of the situation may evoke similar feelings of anxiety, fear, and unpreparedness in your client. Remember, some people like to work with background noise, but others can only concentrate when they have complete peace and lack of distraction. Ask clients which they prefer. If they have no preference, recall the conditions under which you do your own best concentrating, and replicate them for your client meetings.

3. *Understanding.* It is my job to take clients from the starting point, that is the questions, concerns, and issues that originally brought them to my office, and lead them through my analysis to a new level of understanding of their situations and methods of solutions. This makes me a professor, because I can educate my clients; a counselor, because I will advise my clients; and a guide, because I can show my clients

how to proceed and lead them to new levels of accomplishment—roles for which I constantly seek to upgrade my skills.

Illustrating Your Findings for Different Learning Styles

Perhaps you have heard theories that tell us there are multiple intelligences, a term made popular in the works of Howard Gardner, a professor at the Harvard Graduate School of Education. It means people can be proficient at many different things (e.g., music, art, sports, math, science) and have many different learning styles (e.g., linguistic, spatial, or quantitative). Some people prefer one learning style, but most of us use a combination of styles. This is true of my clients.

Often, learning styles differ in couples I work with. Matt and Jessica are longtime clients of mine. Matt is an engineer. He is very well organized and prepares for each meeting to the last detail. I never have to ask Matt about his cost of living or the value of his portfolio—he has that down pat. I do not have to remind Matt to bring in his tax returns or other relevant documents. He loves charts and graphs and enjoys looking at pages of numbers. His goal is to get the most information about his total financial picture. Matt's wife, Jessica, is an art teacher. Her eyes glaze over just as Matt gets gleeful when we discuss their numbers. Jessica is reluctant to ask questions because she feels she is slowing Matt down. Yet, when given the chance, she has lots of things to discuss, such as how the numbers translate into an appropriate lifestyle for them.

In other words, Jessica prefers to skip the backup charts, graphs, and numbers and move directly to the bottom line. Tell Jessica how much to save or how often to plan a vacation, and she will follow through to the letter. She is great at budgeting but needs to have their financial plan broken into smaller segments. When we meet, I allow time for both Matt's and Jessica's learning styles.

Before you meet with your clients, particularly when you have not yet identified their primary learning styles, be prepared to present your information in several ways. If you prepare only an oral plan, that is, you simply discuss your findings without benefit of written material or backup charts and numbers, but your clients learn visually, or prepare only numbers without an accompanying written narrative, but your clients prefer words to numbers, you and your clients may be missing the boat.

Tools I Use to Reach My Clients' Style of Learning

Charts and graphs are visual representations of numerical trends that I want to call to my clients' attention. I use them to emphasize not only happenings in the markets, but also to detail items in my clients' individual lives, such as increases or decreases in income over time. Charts (including pie charts and bar charts) and graphs express my findings simply, clearly, and with great visual impact. For even greater impact, invest in a color printer to make your point.

Schedules and tables of numbers can be difficult for some clients to follow. Simple, clear headings and highlights at significant points in the clients' lives, such as at retirement, can help clarify the meaning of the numbers. I usually incorporate some schedules into the plan, and withhold others that I will distribute if backup information becomes desirable. Since there are few Matts in my practice, those backup schedules rarely see the light of day.

The written narrative is a strong component of my plans and the one I find most of my clients are able to zero in on. In a straightforward conversational style, I explain each point clearly, simply, and without resorting to financial jargon. Just like some national newspapers, my narratives are geared to an eighth grade reading level. At various times, I have had the narrative part of my plan reviewed by a professional editor to make sure I am presenting material in a clear, simple way without retreating into financial double-talk.

An oral presentation is a great way to round out the meeting in conversational style, allowing for verbal give-and-take and questions from the client. While the written document that you have spent so much time preparing seems to be the mainstay of the presentation, for many reasons I believe the true centerpiece is the oral discussion. Presenting the plan orally allows you to stop and start whenever the client has a particular question or area of interest, explain each point to your client's satisfaction, and highlight those items that seem to be of greatest interest. You can summarize and expand on various elements of the plan. Do not be dogmatic—good teachers speak clearly but do not lecture unduly. This discussion is so much the meat and potatoes of my work, that even when I present a plan to a client who is hundreds or thousands of miles away, I send out the written document first and then arrange a telephone conference call of an hour or longer to orally discuss the plan.

Following are five tips to present your plan orally in the most effective way:

1. *Be prepared.* Know all the financial circumstances of your client's life. Be familiar with your findings. You should know your recommendations so well that you barely have to refer to your written material.

2. *Substantiate all recommendations with facts, charts, tables, and schedules.* Keep many of them in reserve for that rare client who wants extra documentation, but do not impose them on clients who have little or no interest.

3. *Know where everything is.* Do not dig and search for papers while the client is waiting. Have it all at your fingertips, perhaps in a file folder on your desk or table.

4. *Have a beginning, a middle, and an end to your presentation.* Start with why you are meeting and what you will cover, including the client's goals, issues, concerns, and circumstances. The middle might comprise the facts in each part of the plan. The end can be your analysis, recommendations, and a summary of all your findings, or a to-do list for the client. You are the discussion leader. You decide how to proceed, and when to spend more or less time on a particular topic.

5. *If you are new to oral presentations and uncertain about your skills, sit down with your secretary, spouse, child, or family pet, and practice, practice, practice.* If no one is available, talk to the bathroom mirror. Join a speakers' group if that helps, because small-group plan presentation is public speaking at its most intimate. How well you present your findings will influence your clients' opinion of the recom-

mendations and how likely your clients are to incorporate them into their financial lives and turn to you for help in the future.

Keep your plans simple. It is your job to present sophisticated concepts in clear, easy terms, adding more information when you think your client is ready to hear it. By the time you reach the plan presentation, you should have offered some numbers (such as a balance sheet and/or cash flow figures) to your client to make sure you are on track. This should not be the first time your clients review their numbers, and they should not be taken by surprise at your findings. Finally, as I tell my prospects when we talk about what their plan will look like, their actual numbers—rent, salary, mortgage, stock portfolio—should be easier to understand than fictitious ones, and should make sense to them.

Goals Section

Following is a restatement of my clients' goals as told to me in our in-person meeting and taken from the clients' questionnaires. These particular clients are a married couple who are getting ready to retire. Some clients have more goals, others have less.

The most important part of this section is that it provides an opportunity to communicate with your clients about their most crucial and personal issues. I want my clients to know that I have heard and understood their goals. Furthermore, I like to remind clients of their goals because keeping their goals foremost in their minds during the plan presentation helps them relate better to my analysis and recommendations.

Your Goals

A. You wish to know if you can retire at age 62 and live comfortably thereafter. You are willing to work until age 65 if that would significantly increase the quality of your lifestyle after retirement.

B. You would like to generate the necessary income from your investments to supplement your Social Security and pension income after retirement.

C. You would like to know how to handle your retirement investment accounts. You also wish to know how best to allocate your investments and which specific securities you should hold.

(Continued)

D. You are considering selling your home at retirement and moving to a smaller home in a warmer climate. You wish to know if that is a good idea for you.

E. Leaving money to your children is not important to you. Yet you wish to know if you can make modest gifts to them during your lifetime.

My Summary

This is the summary that I put at the front of the plan. Each section is developed more fully within the plan document. Again, communication is one of my goals here. I want each client to have an idea of what is coming before we get to an in-depth discussion of each section of the plan.

This summary, in effect, provides a preview of what is to come, in much the same way that an experienced speaker will often tell the audience what topics he will cover. Of course, each client will have different goals, summaries, and life situations.

A Summary Overview of Our Findings

A. Overall, your present and future financial prospects are strong. You should be able to generate the necessary income from your retirement accounts to supplement your Social Security and pension income to support your lifestyle. However, it will likely be necessary to work past age 62 and to slightly lower your cost of living to accomplish your goal. You will be in a stronger financial position if you work to age 65. It will also strengthen your position to earn a modest amount of part-time retirement income.

B. Selling your home and buying a less expensive one in a warmer climate after retirement will help you meet your goals.

C. We have developed a recommended asset allocation for your investment portfolio. It focuses on your retirement assets. We worked from assumptions gleaned from the information you supplied that you prefer a moderately aggressive risk portfolio.

D. We offer you some estate planning and gifting recommendations in that section of your plan.

What to Do

I close my plans with a to-do list that I divide into various sections so my clients do not leave thinking, "That was nice, but what do I do now?" This is the final way I communicate with and instruct my clients in their plan.

I remind clients of what needs to be done, but I do not schedule dates by which each step should be completed or list names of who will execute each step, but I have seen many other planners do this successfully to motivate clients.

The following to-do list applies only to these particular clients, not to all clients, and is intended here as a sample of the kinds of advice I offer my clients. You should adapt your recommendations to your unique style.

To-Do List

Cash Flow Planning
- Your cash flow situation is good. Continue to contribute to your retirement plans, and consider saving assets outside your plans.

Retirement
- You are positioned to enjoy a comfortable retirement if you make some minor adjustments.
- You should plan to work past age 62, retiring at ages 64 and 65, respectively.
- Part-time work income will benefit you during retirement.
- Monitor your situation annually to ensure that you stay on track toward your goals.
- Carry out your plan of selling your home and moving to a lower-cost home in a warmer climate after retirement.

Investments
- Establish a more diversified portfolio that takes advantage of broader asset class categories than you currently are using.
- Redistribute your assets for better diversification and fund selection.
- Review and rebalance your portfolio at least annually.
- Implement the changes in your portfolio that are recommended in your plan.

Estate Planning
- You have new wills and do not face an estate tax problem.
- You should each draw up powers of attorney, healthcare proxies, and living wills.
- Make sure your property titling and beneficiary designations are in order.
- You can gift to your children for special occasions as discussed in the plan.

(Continued)

Overall
- You are on track to accomplishing your goals. The next few years will better help you determine your readiness to retire since your investment returns and your spending and savings will affect your financial position.
- It is wise to review your progress toward your goals annually.

Note: The meat of each client's plan is the cash flow, insurance, tax, investment, retirement, estate, and other sections that fill most of the plan document. Each section of the plan should be tailored to meet the individual needs of your clients. Your analysis and recommendations should be clearly stated and communicated.

Do Not Overload Clients with Information Even If You Are Right

My financial plans start with an overall summary of my findings, which alerts clients to what lies ahead. Then I break the plan into sections: cash flow analysis, insurance, tax, investments, retirement, and estate. I start where the client is now in each area of the plan, talk about their issues, concerns, and goals, state my findings, and lead into my recommendations. I provide the results of my analysis and what I think that client should do, the advantages and disadvantages of taking a particular action if useful to the discussion, and the expected results of the action.

When I present the plan, I tell my clients as much as they seem able to absorb. I never indicate that a client should take an action just because I said so. I explain my reasons for each recommendation. I have done my due diligence in every area of the plan and have backup materials in my files to prove it. That backup documentation was my homework and my way of checking on my own facts and figures. But it is of no more interest to most clients than knowing how the chefs at their favorite restaurants prepared their meals. I let the client's questions and level of interest and understanding determine how deep the discussion on a particular issue will be.

I am prepared with much more material than most clients want, but I do not need to divulge it all at once. Now that I am an expert, I am confident enough to know what and how much my clients are asking for and to give it to them in the right measure.

How can you tell when clients have had enough of a particular topic? Since the presentation is an opportunity for give and take, observe your clients during the meeting. Watch for the following signs of disengagement:

- *Eyes Glazing Over.* Foggy eyes and a tuned-out look mean that you have passed the client's point of interest. Slow down and start again, or adjourn for another day when everyone is fresher.

- *Asking the Same Question Over and Over.* Repeated questions can mean that you are not getting through. Think back to your last response; perhaps it was unnecessarily complicated. Simplify your explanation, ditch the jargon, and call on your patience as you begin again.

- *Silence from across the Table.* No response for a long period of time may mean your client is truly lost. Ask leading questions to find out what the client's comprehension is and bring the client back into the discussion.

- *Unconditional Agreement with All Your Points.* Continual nodding of the head or unquestioning acceptance of everything you say may not signal approval. It may indicate that the client is totally mystified by your plan or your presentation. Worse, it could mean that the client is bewildered by how your information can apply to his life. Go back several points and identify your client's true level of agreement with you. Then restart the conversation from the first point of uncertainty that you detect.

Take control of the meeting. Tell your clients the outcome of your analysis, but do not go beyond their level of understanding, patience, or ability to concentrate. You do not look better and they do not learn more if you keep going past the point of comprehension. Let them tell you by means of their bodily and verbal signals when to go full speed ahead and when to cut back the engines. Fortunately, there is rarely a time limit on your knowledge and expertise. Although you may be eager to impart your findings, if you cannot finish relaying them all in one meeting, step back, slow down, call it a day, and schedule another appointment for phase two of the plan presentation.

Dealing with the Sensitivities of Their Other Advisors

Many times I am asked if my client can bring another advisor to our meeting. Typically, this is an attorney or accountant, generally someone the client has known longer than he has known my firm. I always say yes. There are many good reasons to include other advisors:

- Having another advisor at the presentation helps you learn more about your client and how other parts of the financial life are being handled.

- It makes you part of a team. Assembling a group of advisors makes sense for many people for the following reasons: clarity, smoothness, preparation for future interaction, and avoidance of duplication.

- Another advisor can help interpret your findings to a client you have just met.

- Meeting with another advisor widens your circle of professional acquaintances and puts you in the position of expert in your field. Treat the other advisor with respect, show that you are not a threat to an existing relationship with the client, and involve the advisor in the conversation. If the advisor is good, you may use her services for other clients. Advisors who appreciate the quality of your work may call on you as well.

Client meetings that involve several professionals usually have an extra edge. The client can get a multitude of professional advice delivered in a business-like way with only a little time allotted to social niceties. Issues are likely to be thought through ahead of time, and the conversation is kept to the point and moves ahead in a sprightly manner.

Finally, you have the advantage of another professional viewing your work and bringing any uncertainties, omissions, or problems to the fore. You will get a new perspective on your work, and have a chance to raise and answer questions. Since the meeting will be in your office, you have the home-court advantage. Present yourself well in these meetings, and you will benefit in the long run.

Sometimes, clients want to bring a personal confidant to the meeting. The second-most-asked question about my presentations is, "Can I bring my friend, relative, or colleague?" If the client is on his own, I think it is a good idea for him to bring someone he trusts for support and as a second set of ears. This friend may hear things the client does not hear, particularly if the client is nervous or flustered. And when they leave my office, the client has someone to talk things over with.

My clients occasionally bring along someone who is considerably more financially savvy. Recently, I had a client arrive with her relative, a Securities and Exchange Commission employee. Once we got past the regulatory jokes, we had a full, rich, professional session.

Other times, clients bring someone who does not understand financial concepts any better than the client. Then I might have to work extra hard to explain concepts to two people with different learning styles. Either way, whatever makes my client more relaxed is okay with me.

The Case for or against Taping Plan Presentations

Sometimes clients want to record our meeting. Usually this is to help them remember our discussion. I believe that is a good idea. They can replay the parts of the meeting that confused them, listen in a private relaxed setting, share my findings with their loved ones, and review the steps they are supposed to take to carry out my recommendations.

In favor of taping are calm (the client can listen at home when she is relaxed), ease of understanding (repeating your findings can make for increased clarity), and concentration (the client can proceed at her own pace and focus on important areas).

Against taping—well, I cannot think of a good reason against taping. If you are worried that someone will hear something you tell your client that was inappropriate or incorrect, then you should not have said it, anyway. If you are well prepared for your presentation with all the facts and correct information, this should not be an issue for you. If something you do not know comes up during the presentation, tell the client you will check it out and get back to them.

To answer a question that may be on your mind: No, no one has ever asked to videotape my presentation. Even though I have appeared before television cameras many times, and I do think a videotape might be a good training tool for me and my staff, I think I would feel self-conscious and not have a good meeting. In this case, I think low tech works better for me.

Answering the Same Question More Than Once

Why do clients ask the same question over and over? Do they not understand your explanation? Were they not paying attention to your answer?

There can be several reasons:

- Your presentation went right past the clients. It was not explained in terms that related to their situations. What should you do? Clarify, reframe your answer, and give it to them patiently, clearly, slowly, and in small pieces. I always think it is my fault if I do not communicate a point to my clients.

- Your clients may well know what you mean, but want your reassurance. They may really be asking, "How do I translate this information into my own lifestyle?"

- The clients might not have absorbed all the information the first time. They may need to hear it again just to confirm that they got it, or to sort out what they did and did not understand.

- The clients may want to spend a little more time mulling over a point before moving on. They may be giving themselves the gift of more time and space.

Discuss your concept and explain how it will fit into the client's life. Do not simply repeat what you said before. Try a new way of explaining the issue at hand. Use an analogy—when talking about diversification to someone who cooks, compare your concept to preparing a salad using many different ingredients. For a sports fan, your analogy could center on the different functions of the members of a sports team.

Try examples, such as a story about another client (in which the characters—your clients—remain nameless), or show an example of a specific result of a recommended action for this particular client. Rather than talking about what a good idea it is to save, show your client the end result in real numbers. For example, if the client saves $\$x$ a month for 10 years and invests it at y percent, the end result is expected to be $\$z$. Or, if she wants a $\$25,000$ car in five years, she will need to save $\$x$ a month and invest it at y percent to achieve her desired results. Similarly, the impact of inflation can easily be explained with examples from past decades.

To make sure your client gets your message, reform it, restate it, and slowly try presenting it again. In difficult cases, your explanation may evolve over time. When you are done, check your clients' level of comprehension by asking questions that they should be able to answer. If they are still bewildered, move on to other things. You can always come back to that difficult point later or on another day.

One client of mine, Judith, asked me over and over again how to withdraw monthly sums for living expenses from her portfolio. I explained over and over about the mechanism for having a check sent to her bank from her investment account, but the questions did not end. I realized there was more to her questions than I had thought, so I explained the concept of total return, that is, the various factors that contribute to the growth of a portfolio over time.

Still, Judith's questions didn't stop. When she persisted, I asked another planner in my office, a strong communicator, to explain where Judith's money would come from. Judith seemed pleased by the attention, but the next week her questioning phone calls began again.

I invited Judith's lawyer, Aaron, to come in with her. He had known Judith and her late husband (whom I had never met) for decades. He listened to Judith's questions and to my explanation and turned to Judith and explained the same information in his own words. Following that meeting, I sent Judith articles that addressed the same subject and continued to answer her questions when she phoned.

Finally, many months later, Judith called very excitedly. She said, "I get it!" She had figured out our message in her own way and in her own time with, I like to believe, our support. Do not tell Judith, but several times I had been near giving up. I am glad I did not.

Following is a sample conversation with a client who needs extra explanation. Note that this is a preliminary conversation on the topic. I have condensed it to some of the basics of the subject matter. The concept of total return is a complex one, difficult for many clients to grasp. I have had two-hour roundtables in my office to explain this concept to small groups of clients with the help of visual aids and an extended question-and-answer period.

Client: What happens when I need money from my account?

Planner: Let us determine how much you will need first, and then see how we can get it to you.

Client: But what if I need $2,000 every month?

Planner: No problem. We can have your brokerage firm wire $2,000 to your account each month.

Client: Where will the money come from?

Planner: It can come from a combination of dividends from your stocks, interest from your bonds, and growth in your portfolio.

Client: What do you mean?

Planner: An account can grow in three ways over time. It usually happens with a combination of growth in the value of the securities you own, the dividends your stocks pay out, and interest someone pays you on the bonds you own. Do you have questions about the three ways an account can grow?

Client: Not really. I see what you are saying. I can get money in three ways. And I can take some money out every month.

Planner: Right. You decide when you want it. Will the 15th of each month do?

Client: Yes. That will help me with my monthly bills.

Although the planner has covered a lot of ground in this brief conversation, the client brought the planner back to her original question: How does she get her money out of her account each month? I think it is clear she still has some uncertainty and will ask the planner the same questions again. Next time, the planner could talk about selling off some of her positions versus taking interest and dividends out of the account, and might illustrate with numbers what that specifically would look like in her account.

The client seems most to want reassurance that she has enough money in her account to support monthly withdrawals of $2,000 (the planner has not yet addressed this issue), and to know that the money will get to her bank account in time to pay her bills (which she just might need to experience for a few months to be confident). Appropriately, the planner checked on the client's level of understanding and closed this preliminary discussion on a note of the client getting what she wants, monthly deposits into her account.

Support your explanation by showing your puzzled client simple yet relevant newspaper or magazine articles, and pause from time to time to question your client's level of understanding. Given time, patience, and repeated explanations, eventually he will likely "get it" just like Judith did.

Thinking It Over and Coming Back

When I finish presenting a plan, I always tell my clients to keep a list of questions they forgot to ask, write them down, telephone me with the list at hand, or come back for another meeting. I call those questions people do not ask the first time subway questions, because here in New York many people travel to my office by subway, and it is on the subway after they have left my office that they remember what they should have asked. Fortunately, this is one case in which they do get a second chance. No one is going to cut them off if they come back with more questions. Actually, I like that give and take. The only questions I worry about are the ones that do not get asked.

My goal is to prevent misunderstandings, and to motivate my clients to take action and implement their plans quickly. I do not like to think of my work lying in someone's drawer unused. One of my favorite experiences after presenting a plan was the call I received from a client in Texas. He told me that my plan was on his bedside table and was his "novel of choice." I liked hearing that because it signaled that he was reading and reviewing the plan when he was relaxed, becoming familiar with its contents, and preparing to use it.

Clients can come back to see me about the plan as many times as it takes to make it usable for them. Generally, this is not more than once or twice after the plan presentation, but it can be more times and that is all right.

If the client wants or needs something and I can supply it, I am happy to do so, unless it turns into a whole new project. Some time ago, I was working with Jeff and Lindsay on a plan for their married life together. As soon as I finished the plan, Jeff came in to tell me that he had left Lindsay, was getting a divorce, changing jobs, leaving the city they had lived in together, and looking for a new home. Furthermore, they would be dividing their assets, and planning separately for the future. For this particular case, there was not much I could salvage from their original joint plan, and had to begin work on Jeff's new project—how to structure his life as a single man.

More often, follow-up visits are simply that—more questions pertaining to the original plan. These can be addressed simply and easily by me or someone else in my office who participated in preparing the plan.

A True Partnership

Figure 7.1 shows how the client is central to the planning process. It also illustrates the six components of a plan that will be fully

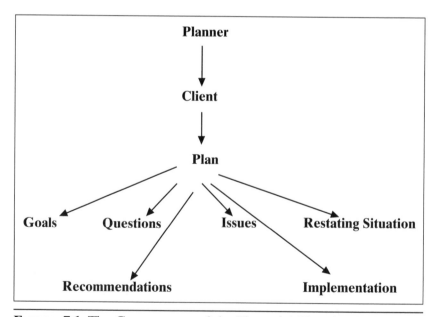

FIGURE 7.1 The Components of the Financial Planning Relationship.

addressed while the project is active: the client's goals, questions, issues, the planner's restating of the client's current situation, the planner's recommendations, and finally, the client's implementation with help or guidance from the planner.

Figure 7.1 shows the true partnership nature of the planner-client relationship. The arrows emphasize the interconnectedness of the people, the problems, and the work. The client is central to the process, the planner heads the network of professionals, and the plan is incomplete until the following occur:

- The client's goals are examined.

- The client's questions are answered.

- The client's issues are analyzed.

- The client's current situation is restated.

- Recommendations are made.

- Finally, the client is instructed how to implement the plan or, in some situations, depending on the nature of the planner-client relationship, the plan is implemented by the planner. Then, and only then, is the planning work complete.

If you feel that you do not have a partnership with your clients, rethink your relationship and make room for your clients in the planning process. Remember, this is their situations, their circumstances, and their work you are doing. Whatever you come up with in your recommendations has to fit into their lifestyles. Forming a partnership with your clients focused on their particular financial issues will help you keep them as clients for life.

Follow Up

After the Plan, What Is Next?

By the time I have finished the financial plan, my staff and I have typically spent weeks poring over my client's financial affairs, income, spending habits, debt, insurance, taxes, investments, pension and retirement plans, and estate planning. I have learned about the client's lifestyle, discussed careers, plans for retirement, future inheritances, and asked about his or her marriage, children, and relationships with other family members. I realize that I might know my clients better than anyone but their closest friends and relatives. It seems silly to dismiss all that I have learned because one large job has ended. I store my knowledge in my client's files, in my database, and in my memory, and keep it ready for future contact.

What is my role now? That depends on my client's need for ongoing advice, desire for periodic checkups, or wish to come see me for future financial and investment decisions.

Most often, my clients and I forge a bond. We both want our relationship to continue. For many clients, I continue to serve as consultant, confidant, cheerleader, and guide. One client, Rita, had long been dependent on her husband for financial guidance.

As the couple aged, she transferred her trust in financial decision making to me. I recommended that she take basic investment courses at her local college to build her knowledge. As her interest in financial matters grew, I suggested that Rita should join the American Association of Individual Investors (AAII) and participate in their monthly meetings. Rita is now treasurer of her local AAII group and has a good command of investment concepts.

Other times, I maintain the role of the expert and continue to have a major impact on the financial and investment decisions that are best for a particular family. When I call these clients with a new idea, I am usually told, "Whatever you think, Karen," or, "I don't know. That's what I hired you for." In cases like these, I will step up to the plate and let the client know what I think is the best course of action based on the family's particular needs and goals, because otherwise the client may be immobilized by indecision.

I particularly enjoy being a mentor to clients who hope to learn more and gain control of their financial affairs over time. I remember one client, Sandra, who I nurtured for many years while she improved her financial knowledge, studied, and took exams. Sandra finally became a certified financial planner. I lost her as a client but gained her as a colleague. Watching Sandra develop her knowledge was like watching a mother bird build her nest, sit on her eggs, return over and over to feed her babies, and then one day fly off when the newly hatched birds were able to leave the nest. I enjoy pushing clients out of the financial nest when they are ready.

I am glad that more and more clients seem to want to participate in their financial decisions. They are asking better questions and frequently want to know the potential consequences of an action before they implement it. I prefer to share the responsibility for making choices with my clients, who are, after all, the people most affected by the decision. I think it is best for people to own their decisions. They have to carry them out and live with the consequences. At the same time, like the baby birds, they are gaining confidence and reaching for independence.

No matter the extent of our relationship, however, I do like to know how I am doing. I occasionally stop to question my clients both verbally and in writing to make sure they are satisfied with the work I have done so far. After the completion of a plan, it is a good idea to have your clients evaluate the financial planning process. They can report how they like what you have done, how well you have explained and delivered the work to them, and how close you have come to meeting their expectations. Your clients should feel free to comment on everything from the clarity of the plan to the binder it is in, from the timeliness of your delivery to the responsiveness of the people they talk to in your office. This simple step can help you work better with them and with future clients.

When I complete a job, large or small, I send my clients a letter and questionnaire (see sidebar "Client Job Completion Letter" below). I use a letter score to allow clients to describe their experiences at my firm. If numbers make you more comfortable, create a number system to elicit the information you would like to have. More than half the questionnaires that my assistant sends out are completed and returned to me within two weeks.

Clients do not have to divulge their names, but their comments

---

Client Job Completion Letter

Dear Client,

It has now been several weeks since we completed your financial plan. We are checking to see whether you have any questions relating to the plan and whether you have begun its implementation.

Since we strive to provide the highest quality work possible, we would appreciate your filling out the form on the following page and returning it to our office.

Please let us know if there is anything you would like to discuss in a follow-up phone call.

Best regards,

(Staff Person's Name)
Client Relations

Work Completion Questionnaire

Please evaluate our work in the following areas. Circle the grade that most closely expresses your feelings: E (extremely satisfied); S (satisfied); N (neutral); D (dissatisfied); VD (very dissatisfied).

L.J. Altfest & Co., Inc. staff's attention to your needs	E	S	N	D	VD
Information communicated clearly in writing	E	S	N	D	VD
Time in getting work completed	E	S	N	D	VD
Clarity of plan presentation by staff	E	S	N	D	VD
Usefulness of financial planning recommendations	E	S	N	D	VD
Ease of implementation	E	S	N	D	VD
Value for money spent	E	S	N	D	VD

Would you recommend L.J. Altfest to your friends/relatives?
Circle: YES   NO

Additional observations and recommendations   _____

_____

_____

Is there anything in particular that L.J. Altfest can do to improve the process?   _____

_____

_____

I would like someone from L.J. Altfest to call me to discuss   _____

_____

Client's name (optional)   _____

Phone   _____

are very welcome. We provide space on the reverse side for additional comments. To increase our rate of response, I enclose a self-addressed envelope. Then, whenever we accumulate a handful of these responses, I meet with appropriate members of my staff to discuss them. My goal is to address any problems we find in these surveys and correct them in order to give our clients as good an experience with our firm as possible. If you receive even one complaint about your style, service, or delivery, it bears looking into. There is always something to learn from a client's comments and some steps you can take to improve your system or services.

If you are preparing a questionnaire, keep it simple so that people do not have to struggle with it, keep it brief so that people do not have to spend a lot of time on it, and keep it objective so people do not feel they are personally insulting you. Two years ago, I received a few responses that said I understood the clients' problems, my work was good, they would recommend their friends to me, but the work had taken longer than they liked. I met with my staff, reviewed our procedures, discovered where the slowdowns were, tightened up our systems, and began to produce plans in about 60 percent of the time it used to take. Now if there is going to be a delay, I always contact my clients to discuss the problem with them, instead of keeping them waiting without giving a reason. That has made a world of difference to me, my staff, and my clients. I am thankful that my clients cared enough to tell me something that could help me work better.

You do not want only your most positive clients returning these surveys. You want to hear the whole story about how your clients view your services. Your goal is to attract as many responses as possible, with complete and accurate information. Quite likely, your response to customer feedback will help you improve your strengths and correct your weaknesses, which will attract new clients to your firm. Your clients are your allies, helping you to make your firm the best it can be. Be grateful for their help, and always take their comments seriously.

Contact Clients Regularly to Check on What They Have Done

After the plan is completed, whose job is it to maintain contact? Should you be reactive and wait for your clients to pick up the phone because you are busy with new projects? Or should you be proactive and keep your clients on a regular contact schedule?

I keep my clients on my mailing list and include them in special events, such as educational seminars, that I offer at my firm. I send them newsletters and think of them when something I know will interest them comes my way.

While staying in touch often depends on clients' needs, their personalities, and your level of service, it is a good marketing tool and an efficient way to make sure that your clients have implemented your recommendations. Although it can be easier to do nothing, being proactive will help you maintain your client base and gain referrals from satisfied customers. Just as you show you are thinking of clients, they will think of you.

Sometimes, keeping in touch can lead you down an unexpected path. Just recently, I called Bill and Patricia to ask about Bill's health, and to find out if they had resolved a recent dispute with Patricia's employer. To my surprise, Bill mentioned that their neighbor, a well-known writer, had just been talking to them about her financial decisions. Would it be all right, Bill wanted to know, if he told the writer to call me. Of course, I was very pleased to know that Bill and Patricia thought so highly of my work, and anticipated the well-known prospect coming to meet me. Would Bill have thought of me if I had not happened to call for an update on their situation? Maybe, and then again, maybe not.

Remembering your old clients is a good way to maintain the connection, show your concern, and be introduced to new clients. For a minimum of time, no cost, and just a small effort, you are fulfilling your advisory role and subtly marketing yourself as well. You may also flatter your clients with your special attention. That good feeling will last a long while.

If you do not know what to say and need a reason to call, check out the local news or economic conditions. Recent events can provide you with a smooth entry into an interesting conversation. Whenever I think about calling a client, and wonder how I can find a reason to call, within 48 hours some issue of consequence to that person crosses my desk, usually in the form of a newspaper or journal article.

Following is a replay of a conversation I had recently with a client whom I had not spoken to in several months:

KCA: Hi, Alison. This is Karen Altfest. How are you?

Client: Karen! I'm fine, so nice to hear from you.

KCA: Have you been having a good summer?

Client: Yes. I just visited my daughter in Ohio. Now I'm getting busy at work, though, because one of my assistants just left and we have not found a replacement for her yet.

KCA: That must be difficult. I was thinking about you recently because I read that your company is merging with a similar operation, and I wondered if you had any questions about what you should do with your retirement account now.

Client: You know, I was just wondering about that. They gave us some choices, and I don't really understand them.

KCA: Why don't you gather all the materials you have received and bring them into my office. We can have a look at the choices available to you.

Client: Great! That is just what I would like to do.

Note that I started with general greetings, moved to soliciting an update on the client's situation, and then brought the conversation around to something that I felt would be of concern to Alison, her company's merger and changes in her retirement plan. Apparently, I pressed the right button. Alison was concerned about this very issue.

This phone conversation began with a loose structure, yet it revealed a real need that this client had. For very little time and effort, I renewed an old relationship and helped my client, Alison, face some important choices. I knew from the moment she answered the phone that Alison was pleased to hear from me. I was glad I had decided to call.

Are They Moving toward Their Goals?

In addition to reaching out via phone calls, I stay in touch with my clients through their annual visits. I invite them in for their annual update by sending a note telling them that it has been a year since their last visit, just like a dentist. The major difference? My note does not have a picture of a toothbrush on the front.

If you do not know what to say in your annual update reminder, keep the next few postcards or letters you get reminding you to come in for an annual checkup. Then take the best of the best and adapt them to your practice.

Your Annual Visit Reminder

Dear Client,

It has now been more than a year since your last visit to my office. Since you were last here, the economy has moved along at a rapid pace, we have elected a new mayor, and oil prices have risen dramatically. Perhaps you have experienced changes in your personal or financial circumstances as well.

This would be a good time to review your financial plan and determine if you are on track toward your goals. Please call my assistant Helen at (212) xxx-xxxx to schedule an appointment for your annual review.

I look forward to seeing you soon.

Sincerely,

Can these annual reminders ensure that your clients will be with you for life? Probably not, but it will put your clients on a regular schedule to evaluate where they are. You will be part of the regular cycle of progress toward their goals. You will be able to monitor their progress and correct their mistakes. In other words, you will become a permanent part of their financial planning process. And they will think of you year after year as they move ahead through life.

Monitoring your clients' progress toward specific goals is part of your job responsibilities. Financial planning is not a hit-and-run situation, but an ongoing process. You should monitor, maintain, and reevaluate the plan over several decades. You can choose to supervise your clients' achievements and prevent a backward slide, or you can teach your clients to monitor their steps to success themselves. But beware. If you aren't actively involved in your clients' financial lives, you are leaving them open to other advisors who might like to take over your job.

If you have not seen your clients for a while, how can you determine what progress they have made? Ask them outright. Come prepared with a list of one-time to-dos from your plan, and a second list of ongoing steps. Then listen to your clients as they tell you about the changes in their lives since your last meeting.

The to-do list will tell you (and your client) what the client has accomplished and what is left to do. The ongoing steps list serves to remind you and the client about the long-term steps necessary

---

Making Sure Clients Are on Track

To-Do List

Action (from Plan)	Date Accomplished	Steps Outstanding
Get new will	May 14	Get power of attorney
Transfer accounts to new broker	September	None
Make changes in account		Still working on it
Buy disability insurance		Call agent

Ongoing Steps

Contribute maximum to company 401(k) plan

Pay down credit-card debt; do not use the cards

Deposit $400 per month into son's college account

Save $300 per month for new car

Eat out less often

Spend less on babysitters

After you review what has been done and what steps are outstanding, draw your client out about other life changes. Following is a sample conversation with your client.   *(Continued)*

Conversation

Planner:	You have accomplished many of the steps we talked about.
Client:	Yes, I was doing well, but now I decided to leave my job and look around for something I like better.
Planner:	Have you given notice at work?
Client:	I have. I expect to be out of there by the end of the month.
Planner:	Do you have any leads for a new job?
Client:	Not yet. Actually, I thought I might freelance for a while. The only thing that worries me is, what will I do for health insurance? I know I can keep my insurance through COBRA, but I don't like the carrier my company uses anyway, and I would rather look for a new policy.
Planner:	Let's see what your needs are, and then I'll put you in touch with an insurance agent who can help you. Meanwhile, keep what you have.

to achieve goals. Finally, the conversation alerts you to changes in the planning situation. Now, with these three sources of information, you can see where the client is in the planning process, what the remaining needs are, and what steps to institute to keep this family on track.

What to Do with Clients Who Procrastinate

I have heard some very creative excuses from clients who do not want to implement their plans. They say they will get started when they come back from vacation, when the kids return to school, after the New Year, after their birthdays, after their in-laws' visit, after they have remodeled the house, after they pay their taxes, and when they get their bonus at work. What can you do with clients like these? Plenty. Following are four techniques that have worked in my office:

1. *Plan an In-Person Meeting.* Set a date when the client has to sit across from you, look you in the eye, and confess to what he has not yet done. Give clients two weeks' notice

when you set up the meeting, which allows them time to take action before coming to your office.

2. *Speak to the Client's Other Advisors.* Call the client's other advisors (attorneys, accountants, insurance agents, brokers, etc.) and set the wheels of implementation in progress. Do not just give out the number of someone your client should see; call that professional and set a time for a meeting. If necessary, you can go along and make sure the meeting happens. Even better, hold the meeting at your place; then you do not have to travel and can be just as effective.

3. *Arrange Conferences by Phone.* Schedule telephone conference calls for you, the client, and the other professionals who will be implementing the work. That way you will not all have to give up a large block of time to get together. If your telephone system cannot handle a large group conference call, ask your telephone service carrier to arrange it. Once you have discussed the major issues and are all on the same track, you can make progress.

4. *Prepare the Materials for Getting Started.* Confront the client with the forms needed to take specific action, such as to open new accounts, inquire about Social Security benefits, or apply for Medicare. Sit your client down at a table in a quiet place in your office, and provide a pen and a glass of water. Walk out, close the door, and check on the client later. I think you will find that the paperwork is moving right along.

Periodic Follow-Up Sessions

How often should you meet with clients after you have finished a project for them? That will depend on the level of involvement they request and the amount of hand-holding they require. Some people want to handle everything themselves. They know what has to be done and expect to take responsibility and carry out the tasks on their own. Others do not seem inclined to do anything by themselves. They lean on you every step of the way.

They may never have handled their finances before, or they may be too ill, elderly, or dependent to want to do it now. You can determine the type of service you are comfortable providing.

At my firm, I offer many different levels of ongoing service. With some clients, I have an ongoing relationship that includes management of their assets and financial advice. These clients can call with questions about how much new car they can afford, which is the best mortgage for them to take, or how much they can spend on renovating their kitchen. Recently, Paula called to ask me if she could leave her job at age 50 (in five more years) instead of hanging in until age 60, which she had originally planned to do. I am running some numbers for her to see if this will work, or if she will have to make adjustments in her lifestyle now or in retirement. Perhaps Paula will have to work a year or two longer to achieve the lifestyle she desires in retirement. The bottom line is I am in a position to know all the relevant factors about Paula's life, and I am glad to get her the answer to her important question.

Harold, on the other hand, does not have assets for me to manage, and since I did a comprehensive financial plan the first year I knew him, he is on his way to saving for future objectives. He comes in regularly for an annual update on his progress. He brings news of changes in his career and personal life, I adjust his plan, and I know I will not see him until a year later. This works well for Harold; he is on target toward reaching his many goals.

Lillian and Ralph pop in to see me only when something major in their lives changes. They came in when Lillian's mother died and left an inheritance, then again when Ralph got a large raise and promotion at work, and yet again when Ralph decided to change careers. Typically, I see Lillian and Ralph about once every two years. That is all the guidance they want at this point in their lives.

I like having different levels of involvement with various clients. I know some clients need me more than others, and I respond to each situation with the appropriate level of service. One problem I do have, however, is answering the question, "How many clients do you have?" I have a large pool of clients. Some I see regularly, some only occasionally, but I know they will turn up again when they need me.

A Typical Update Agenda

An agenda that outlines what you will cover is as useful for your annual update as it is for the first meeting. I do not send out an update agenda in advance of the meeting, but I do have one ready. I tell my clients on the phone what we will discuss and what they need to bring. This includes a recent tax return, a copy of their most recent brokerage account statement, any new information about company payroll or benefits, and a copy of any new legal documents. If the situation has changed dramatically since the last meeting, I ask them to send these documents to my office a week before their appointment. If there have been major changes in their cost of living, I may ask them to fill out a new expense form as well.

I find that many clients have questions they want to ask in the annual meeting, so I spend some of my time on those. Then I proceed to my agenda, which may include:

- Changes in the client's lifestyle
- Changes in the client's income and expenses
- A review of the client's investments, including rebalancing investment accounts
- A discussion of the steps the client was supposed to take after leaving my office last year and what remains to be done
- A new to-do list

Often at this meeting, I have the client write a personal to-do list as we talk. Just like note taking in college seminars, it sometimes makes the tasks more real and easier to remember when the person writes it down. Writing helps some people concentrate and gives them an opportunity to literally see what they do not understand and to raise questions as the meeting progresses.

It is a good idea to type up your recommendations and send them to the client a few days after your meeting. That serves as a confirmation of what you have accomplished in the meeting for your files, a good reminder for your client, an opportunity to reach those clients who learn best by reading material instead of listening, and a good way to stay in touch with clients you wish to keep for life.

Six Problems I Have Seen and How to Solve Them

Not all financial planning situations end smoothly, no matter how careful we are or how much we wish them to end well. Even with the best intentions and most thorough preparation, you might run into some of the following problems:

1. *Where Did She Go?* Much as it astounds me, every year I meet one or two clients with many issues and concerns. They are serious about finding workable solutions to their problems. These clients complete my forms, sign my agreement, pay my deposit, and then disappear. Why would anyone do that? I believe it is a severe form of procrastination. They have decided to do the work, but cannot bear to confront the situation or have it finished. What can you do to bring the plan to completion? Phone those clients, e-mail them, put it in writing, and as a last attempt to get their attention, send them a certified letter. That usually brings them to their senses.

2. *Need Plan—Your Place or Mine?* I have had a few clients over the years who live within commuting distance but refuse to come to my office in downtown New York City. They are typically less than an hour away. If the plan is done and the client will not come to your place, do not engage in a power struggle. Offer to fax the plan or send it by Federal Express and arrange a telephone conference to discuss it. This can be an effective way of delivering your plan, and you will have met your obligations to the client. Moreover, do not be surprised if, once you agree that she does not have to travel, the client decides a short trip to your office may be just the thing!

3. *Caution—New Work Under Way.* Did you ever finish a plan and find that, because of changes in the client's life, major parts of the plan have to be reworked? Recently, one of my long-term clients for whom I had done a plan six months before called to tell me she had just had a buyout at her company, and that now she, the primary breadwinner in the family, was unemployed. She also had a lump sum to invest. When unexpected change happens, keep the parts of the

plan that are still valid, and revise the sections that need altering. Save your time and your client's money by incorporating your knowledge of the client's goals, needs, and family situation into all future planning.

4. *Disagreement Ahead.* Recently, the adult daughter of an elderly client called to tell me her mother wanted to buy a new house, and that a woman in her seventies did not need a house, and I was to tell her mother to forget that idea. The operative words here are "daughter of an elderly client." The *mother* was my client (not the daughter), and I knew how excited she was to be purchasing her dream house. She had the means necessary to buy and support the house, and every right to do as she liked with her money. While being respectful of the daughter, I had to explain that it was her mother's decision and that the two women should discuss it. I even offered my office as an objective meeting place for their conversation.

5. *Changing the Terms of the Deal.* There is an area of the law that deals with contracts. That is not my field of expertise. My attorney tells me that contracts cannot legally be rewritten after the fact, unless both parties consent to amend the original agreement. Why, then, did my client Marjorie, who came in for investment advice for her mentally incompetent mother, keep coming back with more, new questions and problems for months after the plan was completed? She spent hours composing lists of what she wanted to know long after a reasonable time period had elapsed. Each time I tried to fulfill her need for more information, even though it was far outside the scope of the plan she had engaged my firm to perform. Finally, when my staff and I could no longer feel comfortable answering Marjorie's calls and letters, I told her that her approach was unusual and her demands far exceeded those of our other clients. Marjorie called one more time, and then drifted away. I suggest that you attempt to fulfill your clients' requests unless they surpass the limits of what can be considered reasonable.

6. *The Ultimate and Unforeseeable Reason to Make Changes in a Plan.* No matter how well you and your clients plan,

there are some things you cannot foresee. That was the case with Sue, one of my favorite clients. Sue was a responsible psychiatrist in her sixties who was pleasant to work with. We had her plans well in order when Sue called to tell me she had developed an incurable illness. Within months, she was dead. In respect to Sue's wishes, I called a meeting of her three adult children and their spouses. I helped each of them work on their own plans, contacted the attorney for the estate, and oversaw the division of Sue's assets into three separate portfolios for her children. It was my pleasure to help Sue's children get started on the right foot. I wish I could have done more.

Initiating Regular Meetings versus Waiting for the Next Crisis

Just as diversifying a portfolio across investment categories can help reduce fluctuations, ongoing financial counseling can help level out inevitable bumps in the road. Clients who only come in when there is a crisis may be spinning their wheels, trying to get out of a slump. While I like surprises, I do not enjoy problems that could have been prevented with earlier intervention. Regular contact with your clients can help you manage their progress and prevent sudden mishaps. Frequent and regular contact can help in the following ways:

- Prevent crises. If you are involved on an ongoing basis, you can catch changes and problems while they are still small.

- Stick with the program. You, the planner, are the guide. Like checking in with a coach, your clients know they have to be ready for your meetings.

- Prepare for changes and emergencies. Plan for all areas of your clients' financial lives, monitor their progress, and stay on top of things.

- Know where your clients are going. Set their goals and adjust them over time.

- Give clients a will to succeed that they might not have on their own. Your involvement makes up for willpower that might otherwise grow thin at times.

■ Cement your relationship.

Call this system of ongoing involvement preventive mainte- nance if you will. I believe you can help your clients navigate eas- ily through rough waters. Better to stay in touch than to try to stop the bleeding when an emergency occurs.

Crisis Intervention and Counseling

As Sue's family found out when she died suddenly, even with the best-laid plans, crises will happen. You cannot prevent them. What you can do is lessen the effects of the tornado that has rocked your client's world. Within one recent week, some of my clients experienced job loss, serious illness, death of a loved one, or a business setback. One client, Stan, discovered he had a major illness. Returning home from work one evening, Stan began jabbering to his wife in unintelligible syllables. At first, his wife thought he was fooling around. Then she realized that Stan thought he was communicating with her. She called Stan's physi- cian and told him Stan seemed disoriented and confused. The doctor told her to grab a taxi and rush Stan to the hospital.

Stan's brain tumor was removed the next morning, and he has begun the long road to recovery. Stan's wife saved his life with her quick thinking. I am working to ensure Stan's estate planning is in order, talking his wife through some decision making and meeting with the couple's grown children about some financial issues. My contributions are nothing much compared to what his wife did for Stan, but useful nonetheless.

Stan first came into my office on his 70th birthday. He was worried about who would take care of the finances if he was no longer able to do so. Stan's foresight left his family in good con- dition. Like Stan, many elderly men bring their spouses in to meet me so that there will be someone for their wives to turn to in the event of illness or death in the family. That is a thoughtful and loving step to take. I am pleased that Stan and his wife chose me for such an important role.

Although I do not encourage late-night calls to my home, I am available to my clients in their time of need. I am the planner, they are the clients, and although I am sympathetic about their troubles, I do not panic when trouble calls. My job is to remain calm, rational, reassuring, and start the family on the path to securing their financial situation.

Reassuring is one thing I do well, and you can, too. To effectively counsel your clients, you should take note of the psychological component of your clients' reactions to their financial situations. You have probably seen it in your office. The variety I see among my clients includes:

- Optimists like Robert, who always feels what he does will turn out all right. That is a nice way to be, except that Robert is so sure everything will be okay, he sees no need to take precautions, analyze, or plan. He expects everything to fall magically into place.

- Pessimists like Julie, who told me recently that, even though she has two grown, healthy children, a long-term marriage, and a recent inheritance, she spends all her time contemplating how things might suddenly take a turn for the worse. She worries excessively about losing her money and denies herself all but the basics. She worries about her responsible adult children. I once walked in on a conversation Julie was having with my colleague and thought something terrible must have happened to one of her children, but it was just Julie's way of expressing concern for what *might* happen. Julie is married to Robert. Working with a couple with such different personality traits is a constant challenge.

- Dependent personalities like Harry, who wants me to decide everything for him including where he should retire and to whom he should leave his estate. This is out of my realm, but Harry is not used to making decisions and wants approval for each one.

- Independent people like Jim, who calls to report on what he is doing. Jim is a take-charge person who occasionally seeks my advice. There is no point pursuing Jim. He will be in touch when he wants to be.

- Complainers like Lydia. No matter what I do for her, Lydia calls to tell me what she thinks, and it is not pretty. Lydia thinks her friends' portfolios are up more than hers, I do not contact her enough, I contact her too much, and so on. Just recently, I sent a letter about a new investment opportunity to all my clients, explaining the investment and asking those who were interested to check off some information on an attached form. Guess who was the only client who called to ask why I had sent her an inappropriate letter?

- People who never know when to quit like Terry, for whom I recently did some pro bono advising at the request of a local writer. Terry is extremely grateful for all the work I have done for her. She calls and e-mails me frequently to thank me and say how lucky she is to know me. Then she introduces another problem. After two months of analyzing her situation and answering many complex questions, I am planning to tell Terry that she can call me in a year for an annual update.

If you have been in practice awhile, you probably have a variety of these and other personality types among your clients. I was once identified incorrectly in a newspaper article as a financial planner with a Ph.D. in psychology. Although that is not true (my degree is in history), I have learned to hone some psychological instincts to be able to work with clients of all types.

When you encounter clients with difficult personalities, what should you do? Explore their backgrounds through your questions, see how they feel now and why they developed that way, and over time show them the reality of their situations. Remember, their feelings are valid even though their conclusions may not be on target. Do not judge, do not be impatient, do not argue. Do use empathy, patience, and a knowledge of their situations to straighten out their inappropriate assessments.

Consulting for All Seasons

To be an advisor for all seasons, be flexible enough to allow for many situations and come up with creative solutions to your clients' problems. Figure 8.1 shows the extent of your clients' needs and your role in arriving at solutions to specific situations.

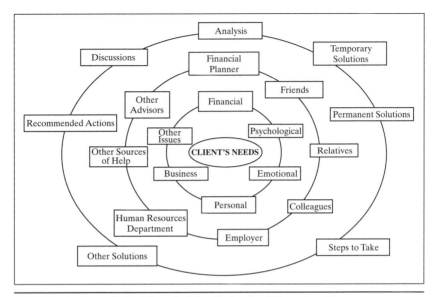

FIGURE 8.1 Client's Needs in the Planning Process.

As the diagram illustrates in the innermost circle, the clients' needs are central to the planning process. These needs will encompass more than the financial area, as you can see in the second ring. The third ring shows that you are not supposed to solve all your clients' issues alone. You may have help from many sources. Finally, the fourth ring illustrates the steps that are inherent in problem solving for your clients' lives.

The Media Is the Message

How to Get Started with the Media

Perhaps you have picked up a magazine, read a financial expert's opinion, and thought, "I can do that." Or you have seen an article on a financial topic and thought, "The reporter should have mentioned X, Y, or Z." Good for you. You are showing the right instincts for working with the media. The first qualification is to know your stuff. The second is a desire to use your knowledge to inform others. Now you have to act on your instincts.

Do you have what it takes? Characteristics that might interest the media include:

- *Knowledge of a particular topic.* By definition, an expert has special understanding of and information about a subject. If you are not yet an expert, then read, study, learn, and make yourself into one.

- *An interest in explaining and educating.* If you love to teach, you will do better with the media.

- *A clear way of speaking and expressing ideas.* Do away with professional jargon; it will confuse, not impress.

- *Enthusiasm about your topic.* It is always more fun to listen to someone who cares about the subject at hand.

- *Promptness and reliability.* Timeliness is of the essence in this realm.

- *A professional appearance.* Mother was right—neatness counts.

- *Patience in your responses.* You may have to explain things more than once.

- *New ideas.* Bring the reporter a new idea he or she can use in an article, and you may well be friends for life.

- *Up-to-date information.* In this fast-paced world, financial information changes rapidly. Do not bring the reporter last year's news.

- *A lively style of delivering your information.* Try to present your knowledge in an interesting and absorbing manner.

If you have some of these characteristics and can work to develop a few others, you are on your way to being a strong candidate for the media. Knowing that you have what it takes, how can you get the media to be interested in your opinions? First, realize that the members of the media interview experts every day. They have their favorites, but they are always in search of new sources of professional opinions. Sure, when big news breaks they will look to tried-and-true sources of information. But when they have more time, they are very interested in beefing up their Rolodexes. It is possible for you to become a trusted media source.

Next, give the members of the media something to work with. When I was a teenager, I had a friend who used to say that she had to go out to meet people because her next boyfriend was not likely to come down the chimney. Similarly, you have to offer something to get the media to notice you. Compile a list of reporters who cover topics that you are an expert in. It is better to have a small, accurate list than a large inappropriate one. Develop an interesting newsletter and send it out to the people on your list. If your information is timely and interesting, people will respond by calling you, interviewing you, or asking if they can use some of your material. If you do not get instant feedback, do not give up. It may take awhile, but if you give the members of the media information that is useful to them, they will follow up.

I do not find press releases to be as valuable as one may think. Press releases are great when they come from famous people, large companies, or are about very important events. For others that fall under that radar screen, personal letters, individual meetings, and new ideas are far more likely to stand out in a crowded field.

If you do not know anyone in the media but want to get started, contact your professional organizations. Many professional groups have media opportunities that they share with their members through speakers' bureaus or through the association's e-mail.

Do you attend professional conferences? So do members of the media. If you are a speaker or panel member and have something new, educational, or controversial to say, you might pique the interest of a newsperson. Come prepared with your cards, and make sure your write-up in the speakers' section of the conference binder includes the name and location of your firm.

You can also get to know some writers over time by responding to articles they have written with your comments and expertise. I do not believe criticizing someone's writing is the way to make lasting contacts, however, so go easy on your points. Be upbeat, helpful, and constructive, not destructive.

Urge your professional associations to hold media roundtables, in which a panel of media members share their needs and advice with you and your colleagues. Listen to what they say, and take the opportunity to introduce yourself either at the end of the presentation or in a letter afterward.

Finally, take a chance and write to the producer (not the host) of a television show that is taped locally, suggesting an idea for a program. Remember, some shows air every day and need a constant supply of experts to comment on the markets, the economy, and other financial issues. I once proposed doing a show about female investors to a major station and found myself appearing as a guest on that station within two weeks. It was great fun talking about something I enjoy so much.

Gaining Credibility in an Incredible World

There is an old saying that people are only supposed to be in the papers three times in their lives: when they are born, when they marry, and when they die. However, our fast-moving world has changed. There are many reasons you may want to be in the press. For example, appearing in the press as a financial expert can help you grow your business, win recognition in a competitive world, and gain credibility. Name recognition can make you stand out among your colleagues. Finally, being in the press can help you differentiate your firm and spread your professional message.

Like me, you probably have a message about your firm, your style, or your beliefs that you want people to hear. I want people to know that I am a fee-only financial and investment advisor, that I do high-quality financial work for my clients, that I work especially well with women and their families, that I guide people toward a comfortable retirement through understanding their goals and managing their investment portfolios, and that I, along with my husband, have a firm of bright, talented, competent, caring professionals.

If you do not have a message that you want to get out about your services and your firm, start to develop one. Write down the things you do, the things you are most proud of, the things you want to communicate about yourself to others, and the things you would like to be known for. This process will help you isolate what it is you do that is special. And it will help you begin to talk about your business to others.

Try to be accurate about your business. Many advisors say they can do more than is true. One planner has unknowingly sent me clients. Why? Because she promises a certain quality of work but does not finish her projects on time or answer her clients' calls. How do clients and prospects differentiate planners who will deliver and those who will not?

A truth of our society today is that most people give credibility to what they read in the newspapers, hear on the radio, or see on television. That larger-than-life aspect of the media lends credibility to people, companies, or advice that appears in print or on screen. Appearing publicly gives you a seal of approval. But here is a warning: The credibility effect is short-lived because there is always another expert waiting in the wings. Nonetheless, the media can help you get your message out, and repetition of your message will keep it fresh in the public's minds.

Working with the media reminds me of the barter system. You give them valuable information and experience; they give you public exposure. You are their expert advisor; they are your window to the world. I find when I am on television, my colleagues, clients, and friends get very excited. I have run into people who told me they were vacationing in India, in England, or were on an airplane when they saw or read about me and were so pleased to see someone they know from home.

People I meet for the first time tell me I look so familiar they think we have met. I think they must have seen me on a television program. People are always watching, listening, and reading. They notice your face and, with a little luck, may remember your name and take the trouble to look for your phone number.

I am not certain, however, that weeks later they remember the words. Therefore, it helps to have a short, memorable statement (known as a sound bite) ready, and repeat and repeat and repeat the message, always making it new and framing it in a way that is appropriate to the question at hand. People who already know you will feel confirmed in their good opinion of you; those who do not yet know you may want to meet you.

You will widen your net of contacts over time. *Note:* There are some people out there who will consider you fair game once you go public. Beware when a caller gushes, "I just saw you on TV. I cannot believe I am really speaking to you." Do not let flattery turn your head. It is not really that exciting to speak to a minor television expert. After all, you are not Warren Buffett or Alan Greenspan. These hangers on will typically take as much time as you give them, but rarely become clients. Somehow, just rubbing elbows with you (either in your office or over the phone) seems to be enough to satisfy their need to reach out to a celebrity. But who knows? Once you hang up, they may phone the next person who was on television after your interview.

Presenting Yourself to the World

Do you want people to think of you professionally as:

- Street-smart
- Financially savvy
- Cool
- Good-looking

- Humorous

- A nice person

You can choose one or more answers from this list and set out to appear any way you wish in the media. But unless you behave very professionally, you may not be invited back. I believe that as an expert I am not a vaudevillian, a Marx brother, a movie starlet, and am not supposed to be overly cool. I leave all that to other folks. In my professional life, I prefer being financially savvy above all else, and I do my best to fulfill all that implies.

To me, being financially savvy indicates that I should present myself in interviews and on television as serious, well-informed, up-to-date on financial and economic issues, helpful, well-spoken, and conservatively dressed. I do not let the seriousness of my topic drain me of all humor, however; I enjoy a smile, a casual exchange of conversation, or a bit of wit as well as anyone. A smile looks particularly good on television, and an amusing aside or a personal remark may help a reporter enjoy the dialogue and form a relationship with you.

I do not try to compete with the politicians, the movie stars, or the world-class athletes who appear on the same show. Actually, sometimes we meet in the greenroom where guests congregate before the show. Those more famous guests usually take the opportunity to ask me financial questions.

If you are a guest on television, try to look your best. Everything is magnified in television close-ups, even windblown hair, stained shirts, or smudged makeup. Make sure you look and feel great, and you will come across very well. Sit in a becoming position, face the host—do not look from camera to camera or at any activity off the set—and respond to questions in a straightforward, clear manner. Answer each question directly. If you do not know an answer when you are in front of a live camera, answer with a related statement. For example, if the interviewer asks about using a specific trust as an estate planning tool, you can say, "I'm not familiar with that trust, but many people find that this other trust works well for the following reasons." Then elaborate with helpful information.

Try to get information from the show's producer about the topic, length of your segment, seating arrangements, and who else will be on the show. Will there be questions from callers, for which there is really no way to prepare? Are you expected to be expert in one segment of financial advice? Is there a topic of the day? I was called on the day the Dow reached 10,000 for a spot on a show about hitting that impressive number. I knew what the interviewer would ask, and I had time to think about how I would respond. Other times, however, the show is more general and questions can cover many areas.

Even when you are given a topic in advance, things do not always work out. One time, I was called to do a show about women and money, one of my favorite topics. It was a two-hour segment, but I was not worried. I knew I had plenty to talk about. When I arrived at the studio, I discovered I was part of a three-person panel that was going to discuss estate planning techniques. Even then, I kept hoping that the topic of women and finance would come up, but of course it never did. We talked about estate planning, wills, trusts, and many other issues for which I had not prepared. Fortunately, it went well (although two hours of not being able to scratch your nose does seem long). The moral of the story is try to get as much information as possible, prepare as well as you can, but do not be surprised no matter where your interview goes.

If you are uncomfortable on television, take lessons from an expert. Many colleges have continuing education classes where they will let you practice public-appearance skills in front of a television camera and then play back your appearance so you and your classmates can offer a critique. There are also groups such as Toastmasters International that can help you gain public-speaking experience. To learn more about them, visit their Web site (*www.toastmasters.org*).

If you are not ready for prime-time television, try to get yourself on some no-name cable channel where people and small companies produce their own shows. These are easier to find than you might think, and since you know fewer people will be watching, you can relax in front of the camera and gain valuable experience. You will then be ready when the networks call.

When you speak on the telephone to reporters for the print media, you do not have to dress in any particular way, but you should have your professional voice and your expert hat on. You can be more relaxed because there are no lights and cameras. You typically will have more time to formulate your answers. You may even be able to research your answers and call the reporter back.

There are rules of media courtesy and professionalism that you should observe over the phone. Take the interview seriously, be prompt and professional. Observe the reporter's deadline. Speak clearly, answer professionally, listen to the extent of the question and offer to call back at a mutually convenient time with the precise answer. I take notes during a phone interview so that I have the full scope of the question written in front of me. Do not try to answer with off-the-cuff remarks. Being flip will not get you into the media. Being professional, however, may get you on the reporter's list for life.

How to Be a Good Guest

To be the kind of guest everyone wants to invite back for another visit, mind your manners just as you would in someone's home. Take heed to the following list of dos and don'ts:

Do Think Before You Speak. Even though there is not much time, know what you are going to say before you say it. If necessary, give yourself more time by asking the host to repeat the question, or you can repeat it in your answer. Repeating the question can take the following form:

Host: Is it better to take Social Security when you are 62 or 65?

Guest: There are reasons why some people should take Social Security at 62 while others would do better to wait until they turn 65.

This has the advantage of slowing down the process and giving you time to formulate your answer.

Do Think in Terms of Main Points. No one will remember all that you say. Help your audience by keeping your information simple and straightforward. Think in terms of main arguments, lists, and top five reasons. If you plan in advance, you can even ask the show's producer to run a list of your top five points on the screen as you speak. Visual aids can help the audience walk away with your most important points.

Do Prepare a Brief, Pointed Summary Statement. When I know the topic in advance, I prepare a few notes and read them in the taxi on the way to the interview. I have an idea of what I want to say and, if possible, the thought I want to leave the audience with.

Do Have Some Rules of Thumb. Rules of thumb are easy for you to list, simple for an audience to absorb, and often useful to apply. They are a good tool for interviews. For most financial advisors, these will not just appear in your mind during the interview; think them through in advance.

Do Have Brief, Illustrative Stories. Stories set us apart from people who do not actually work in the field, but have only studied it. Our practices give us access to human stories every day. Change the names and some of the circumstances, then use the story to drive a point home.

Do Prepare Some Meaningful Comparisons. Sometimes a financial point can be made clearer when you explain what the alternative might be. For example, if you are talking about the tax advantages of municipal bonds, you might have a comparison that includes corporate bonds, government bonds, or certificates of deposit depending on what point you are making.

Do Bring Your Business Cards. Sometimes, members of the media will misspell your name, give you an incorrect title, or reverse the digits in your phone number. To help them, and to be prepared for new contacts, fill your pocket with your business cards so that you do not have to fish for them when you are asked for one. Even if you are not asked, when you meet the show's producer offer your card.

Do Not Chat Aimlessly. You are there to explain but not necessarily expound. Most television shows offer your advice in an interview or question-and-answer format. This is not an opportunity to lecture.

Do Not Interrupt Your Interviewer. As the host, your interviewer will set the tone for the show. Your job is to support him or her, not to outjockey the host.

Do Not Fidget. Moving too much, crossing and recrossing your legs, folding and unfolding your arms can make you look nervous. It can also take attention away from what you are saying to what you are doing. Shake out your arms and legs before you get on the stage set; then forget about them.

Do Not Giggle. While it can be very nice to smile, it is not as nice to giggle. Acknowledge your host's remarks with a cheerful look, but do not spend airtime chuckling.

Do Not Pause for Long Periods of Time. Short pauses in a conversation can seem very long on television. While you might need time to format your answers, keep in mind that airspace needs to be filled promptly.

Do Not Use Phrases Such As "You Know What I Mean." Meaningless phrases with no content detract from your answers. Let the teenagers use "like" at the start of every phrase. You stick to the information you want to convey.

Do Not Give Flip Answers. It is not endearing to give funny answers to serious questions. It may even come across as rude or uncaring to your audience.

Most important, be flexible. This list illustrates the variety of events you should be prepared for. Sometimes, you will have to wait much longer for your spot than you were told, and you may even be bumped from a show altogether. Other times, the important point you saved for the end of the interview may never be seen or heard on television. Or the host may change the topic of the show altogether. Do not complain and do not let last-minute changes throw you. Remember, you were chosen for the show because you are an expert. Learn to go with the flow and respond happily to the task at hand, even though the rules may change as the interview evolves.

Keep in mind that if you look good, the host looks good, too. Do your part to make the show a success, and you will find the media knocking on your door more often.

Do Not Get Caught in a Trap

Sometimes, a reporter will ask you about someone who did something illegal or unethical, or about a colleague you just plain do not like. I do not believe in bad-mouthing anyone. Sidestep the issue if at all possible. If you are on the spot and feel compelled to comment, say something noncommittal such as, "I really am not familiar with the quality of her work."

In the same way, when a prospect comes to my office and says, "I am considering using your firm or the one down the street," I generally say that I have heard it is a very good firm. Of course, if I have heard only negative things about that firm and want to alert the prospect, I would probably say that at the meeting with this firm the prospect should be sure to ask about their experience, credentials, fees, or whatever else may be relevant.

Being negative about someone in your field can come back to haunt you. And going public with your negative feelings may even be libelous. I think this is one time when you will do well to take the high road, say you do not have enough information to comment, and move on.

Helping Reporters Do Their Job—Listen to What They Need

Reporters usually begin by asking if their call is coming at a good time for you to speak. If you cannot give more than a couple of minutes, schedule another time to speak at greater length. I find most reporter calls take from 5 to 20 minutes. Rather than short-changing the reporters, be up front and schedule a better time to speak.

In the first call, try to establish the reason for the call and the parameters of the information the reporter seeks. If the reporter is calling about people who are in debt, I ask if she means mortgages, credit-card debt, personal loans, student loans, or anything else. I want to know if she means one-time debt or continuous debt and if she is looking for debt above a certain dollar amount. When reporters ask about my own clients, I check for the profile they are after—for example, are they looking for information about people at a certain financial level, in a particular age group, who are single or married, with or without children, or do they want to know about couples with high income, or low earnings, or one- or two-career families. The more I know, the better I can help.

Following is a sample conversation with a reporter:

Reporter: Hi, Karen. This is Cliff Jones of the *Big City Eagle*. Do you have time to talk?

KCA: Hi, Cliff. I have a few minutes now and then I am free after 2:00 P.M. tomorrow. Are you on deadline?

Reporter: Not this time. I have a week for this story. Let me tell you what it is about.

KCA: Sure. Go ahead.

Reporter: I am looking for information on a new product that I hear banks are offering. It is a high-paying savings instrument, like a certificate of deposit, only you cannot keep it less than 18 months.

KCA: I have heard of that, but I do not have any clients who actually own one. I can ask around and get some information on it, though.

Reporter: That would be very helpful.

KCA: Will 2:00 P.M. tomorrow be okay?

Reporter: Yes, I will call you then. Thanks for your help.

KCA: You are welcome. I will talk to you tomorrow.

In this conversation, I offered to do research to help the reporter. He described the financial product he was concerned with and told me his time constraints. We agreed to speak again the next day. I consider this agreement as binding as a contract. I expect to keep my part of the bargain by checking with some colleagues in my office and calling people I know at a few banks. When the reporter calls back, I will inform him about the benefits and drawbacks of the product he inquired about.

Could he go directly to the banks himself? Certainly, and he probably will as part of his research. But he will not filter the information in the same way as a financial services professional. With my experience and knowledge of my clients' needs, I will bring a new perspective to the issue. Also, the reporter often needs to use credible experts as sources for the story. Finally, the reporter probably wants an expert to confirm, expand, or challenge the information he already has. Sometimes, you can help a reporter integrate information and know the best questions to ask. You can take the reporter's knowledge a step further if you are willing to do a little research. Then you will be a valuable resource and ally for the reporter, and, like elephants, reporters never forget who helped make their job easier.

To Let or Not to Let Reporters Speak to Your Clients—That Is the Question

Many financial planners have told me they would never ask their clients to appear in the media because it might displease them and disturb the status quo. Since many reporters call specifically to find an ideal person for a story, I try to oblige. I do ask some of my clients if they would like to be in the press if an opportunity arises. I have found in my practice that some clients think it is great fun to be in the news.

Of course, since I know my clients so well, there are some I would never dream of asking. I make a mental note of who thinks it is fun, has spoken to me about my appearances in the press, and of those who would never go public. Actually, I am thinking of adding a question about speaking to the media in my financial planning questionnaire the next time I update it. It may read, "If the opportunity arises, would you be willing to speak to a member of the press about your financial situation?"

When reporters call looking for clients to speak to, I ask what they are looking for. They typically have a particular age, gender, income, investment experience, family situation, job situation, marital status, and financial savvy in mind. I try to match my clients with the reporter's wish list. No need referring a 60-year-old couple with two children to a reporter seeking a 40-year-old couple with no children. If I cannot find the right client in my database, I may ask my employees if they have a friend who fits the profile. This has worked out well many times. My receptionist enlisted her boyfriend to speak to the press, and a colleague got his friend to be on television. Of course, I then tell the reporter that my referral is not a client but someone a staff member knows. The reporter is generally glad to have an appropriate candidate to interview.

Once, I even referred my father-in-law to the *New York Times.* The reporter had called looking for elderly investors who watch their investments carefully, and I mumbled something about my 90-year-old father-in-law who kept the television tuned to money shows all day. The reporter asked if he could meet my father-in-law and watch a money show with him. I asked my father-in-law who thought it sounded like fun, and ran it by my husband (because it was his father). Then, after getting the okay, I made the match, and it was a good one all around. The article gave much coverage to my father-in-law, and the reporter called to thank me for the introduction. Many people read and enjoyed that article, including friends, clients, colleagues, and an old business associate of my father-in-law who had not seen him in 25 years. They arranged a dinner together. If I cannot find a good match, I always call the reporter back to say so, rather than let the matter drift away.

To decide whether you should offer your clients media opportunities, consider:

- Your client typically will *not* have to divulge her income or assets.

- Many people find it fun to see themselves in the press.

- Most people like talking about themselves.

- Clients' friends and families love to see them in the press or on television.

- Your clients will have a nice souvenir of the event—a tape or copy of a newspaper or magazine, and you can go that extra mile and frame it for them.

- Most reporters will respect the level of privacy your clients want, but that should be cleared in advance.

I recommend that you call only those clients who meet the reporter's criteria and have had an experience similar to the one the reporter is looking for. Let your clients know that speaking to the press can be fun, but it is entirely their decision. Assure them that you will continue to like them and do their work whatever they decide. I think you will find many of your clients will accept the opportunity to speak about their experiences.

Building Your Business One Media Relationship at a Time

If you think you will be in the press and your business will explode, you are probably wrong. If you think you can start making contacts, expand your network of relationships one at a time, be supportive of the media, and make small gains in your business over a long period, you are probably right.

Reporters are smart, interesting people whom I truly enjoy talking to and having dinner with. I am happy to take time out of my busy week to return media phone calls, hunt down information, and offer my opinions on many and varied financial topics.

I have instructed my staff to let me know whenever someone from the media is on the phone. I frequently stop what I am doing to take a phone call from someone in the media, or return the call as quickly as I can. If I cannot take the call, my receptionist asks the reporter if he or she is on deadline. Then I can gauge the urgency of the call. I do not discriminate among reporters from various publications. I have found that media people know other media people, and that they move around more frequently than many other professionals. So the reporter from *Small Town Paper,* USA last month may be at *Big City Press* next month.

Local papers can actually be best for helping you build your business. If you are in a national publication, it looks nice in a frame on your credibility wall, so frame those that have the most impact and put them in your waiting room or over your desk. But you may not get much interest from prospects across the country. They generally prefer to work with someone nearby. Get to know your local reporters and make yourself available to them. When your name appears locally, the phone should start to ring, one prospect at a time.

Twelve Rules of Working with the Media

1. *Be Responsive.* Return media calls within two hours even if it is just to find out what the reporter needs, when the reporter needs it, and to set up an appointment to talk again.

2. *Instruct the Media.* Help the reporter get the message across. Be an educator; inform the media. Tell them what they need to know so they can pass it on to their readers or viewers.

3. *Do Not Waste Time.* If you cannot help a member of the media, say so. Do not string interviewers along, promising to help if you are unable to. You will be off their list faster than you can say, "Stop the press!"

4. *Beware of Going Public.* Say only what you would like to see in print. Do not tell reporters things that are not meant for publication. Journalists write what they hear. They do not want to worry about sorting out what they can or cannot use in their stories.

5. *Do Not Ask Favors.* Your job is to help the media, not to add to their hectic load. Giving is better than receiving for this relationship.

6. *Expect Anonymity.* Do not expect to see your name in lights each time you speak to a reporter. I remember telling a reporter everything she needed to know about college planning. When the story appeared, there was my advice, but not my name. No problem. The writer has quoted me several times since then, each time with full attribution.

7. *Do Not Make Demands.* Do not ask for copies of the work. This is a rule I generally follow because I can usually tape the show or buy the publication. I break this rule only if I think I will appear prominently in the article or on the television show and have no opportunity to purchase a copy or tape the program, such as an association publication that is sold to members only. As a backup, find a company that tapes shows professionally and will sell you a copy of the part of the program you want to keep.

8. *Prepare for the Long Road to Stardom.* Do not think this will make you rich and famous. If you think every time your name appears you will be famous as a movie star, remember financial advisors are not that interesting. When I was named planner of the month by *Mutual Funds* magazine in June 2000, I received only a few calls. My favorite was from a reader who assumed I would be happy to analyze his complex portfolio and make recommendations at no charge

to him. The rest of my public must be waiting to call until my photo appears on a Wheaties box.

9. *Admit What You Do Not Know.* Mark this down as one of the most important rules to remember. If you do not know the answer to a reporter's question, you cannot fake it, so do not even try. Misleading a reporter will lead to ill feelings. You will be found out and dropped like a hot potato.

10. *Exercise Reliability.* Do what you say you will do; if you make a promise, deliver. Reporters count on you to keep your commitments.

11. *Know There Are Plenty of Other Fish in the Sea.* You are not the only expert around. Reporters may call you and 10 other experts with the same question, but they expect you to be responsive and reliable. I always call back, even if just to say I could not find the information a reporter wanted.

12. *Do Not Volunteer Unless You Are Willing to Take On New Tasks.* Building relationships with members of the media will involve time, effort, and preparation on your part. If you do not have the time, you will have to make some in your busy schedule, putting the media above some of your other responsibilities. If this is more commitment than you are willing to take on, working with the media may not be your thing. If you are willing to go the extra mile, however, you can form relationships that will last for life.

CHAPTER

10

Service Is Key

Do You Like Doing Social Work? If So, You Have an Advantage

I often think of myself as a financial social worker. I spend so much time hand-holding for my clients, handling their emotional distress, listening to and helping them resolve personal issues, I feel I can claim that title honorably. Lucky for me, I enjoy helping my clients find solutions to their problems. I like people and often find their personal stories compelling. I am patient with my clients and have an innate desire to help people. These personal attributes help me get through my busy week in good spirits.

If you do not like spending your time talking to people, learning about them, and solving their problems, you may be at a disadvantage. Recently, one of my clients told her doctor about a personal problem. His politically incorrect answer was, "Are you complaining again?" Sarcasm will not play any better with your clients than that doctor's did with his patient. Genuine empathy for people and their situations is hard to fake. When you are interested in a personal story, your concern is evident and you reap the added advantage of having it stick in your mind. Then, when a client turns up unexpectedly you do not have to refer to your computer notes to ask, "How is your brother recovering from his operation?" or, "Did you finalize the sale of your house?"

How can you tell if you have the personal characteristics that will turn you into a supersympathetic financial planner? Your answers to the following questions can guide you:

- Do you like to socialize?

- Do you enjoy meeting new people?

- Are you interested in your clients' lives?

- Would you rather spend your time in a group or alone?

- Would you prefer to talk on the phone or read by yourself?

- On your last night out were you an active participant or a passive viewer?

If you answered yes to numbers 1–3, and selected the first of the two possible choices for numbers 4–6, you probably have the right stuff to qualify as a financial hand-holder. Like me, you probably do not mind getting wrapped up in your clients' successes and woes, think about them long after the lights are off at your office, and truly care what happens to each one of them. If not, you can be a very competent and successful advisor, but it might serve you well and give you an extra edge to develop some people skills. Even if you are more comfortable talking numbers than family, you can make an effort to do better without changing your personality or neglecting the work you consider so important. You will find very quickly that your clients want to work with professionals who are responsive to them.

If you wish to improve your client skills, there are several steps you can take:

- Enroll in continuing education programs that enhance the way you communicate with your clients.

- Concentrate on clients who truly interest you, perhaps teachers, police officers, entrepreneurs, athletes, or actors. If you feel comfortable with a particular group, the conversation should flow more easily.

- Promise yourself that you will ask clients two personal questions before they leave your office, and listen intently to their answers. If you have no questions in mind, think them up before your meeting. Some suggestions are:

Where are you vacationing this summer?

How old are your grandchildren?

Where do your children live?

How long have you lived in your present home?

Each question should lead to others. If a client is going to Alaska this summer, ask if it will be the first trip to that part of the country. Then ask if the client is taking a cruise to Alaska or travelling by airplane.

If a client says his granddaughter is turning five, ask if she will be in kindergarten in the fall. Then ask if she is excited about the coming school year. If your client says the children live across the country, ask if they visit often. Then ask when the next visit will be. If a client says that she has lived in her home for 20 years, you can ask how the neighborhood has changed since she first moved there. Then ask if the client is planning to stay in that house after retirement.

Build on the information from each answer when you formulate your next question. That will carry the conversation to a deeper, more personal level. Feel free to put something of yourself into the conversation, such as, "I was in Alaska five years ago. It's lovely." Remember to show your genuine interest by listening well when your client responds.

Your concern will quite likely awaken a stream of confidences from your clients and an added appreciation for you and your personal service. Your clients were probably hoping you would want to learn more about them.

Often I cannot believe the personal things people I hardly know confess to me. I have heard everything from "I am a 40-year-old divorced attorney, but I've never had my own bank account" to "My uncle abused me when I was a teenager" to "My twice-divorced 75-year-old father is supporting two different women in two apartments downtown." These unsolicited pieces of information demonstrate that people have an innate desire to share intimate details of their lives even with new acquaintances.

I have come to expect my clients to tell me about their personal circumstances, but I am still surprised when someone I have just met at a conference or cocktail party tells all about his financial life in the elevator on the way to the lobby. That happens very often and sometimes leaves me close to speechless. I think it is akin to meeting a doctor at a dinner party and telling her all about your appendectomy on the way out, or admitting to a lawyer you have just met that you do not have a will. Our profession reminds people of their shortcomings in the financial area; admitting them seems to have a cathartic effect for some people. I believe discretion is called for in these situations. I have learned to diplomatically answer, "Oh, really?" or to nod my head and refrain from giving spontaneous advice to people I do not know and may never see again.

Even with my own clients, I never lose sight of the fact that I am not really a social worker, however, and generally limit my advice to my area of specialization. If clients persist with queries in other areas, I try to put them in touch with a professional who can help them. I have developed a wide network of contacts in many fields whom I call on when their expertise can be helpful. For example, when a longtime client, Adam, came to me with his problems finding the right nursing home for his mother who has Alzheimer's, I put him in touch with a geriatric-care manager who specializes in placing elderly people in appropriate living situations. When a new client, Esther, told me she could not find a nice apartment in her price range, I introduced her to a real-estate agent who specializes in midlevel apartments.

If you are a take-charge individual who does not generally get involved in a situation unless you personally can take a specific action, let your referral network be your proxy. Sometimes, referring clients to the appropriate professionals can be your way of providing additional service. Other times, your role can be just to listen and express your understanding or concern at the magnitude of problems that face your clients. Very often, that is enough.

When you meet new people ask them what they do, collect their business cards, and begin to form your own referral network. Feel free to interview other professionals before you use them. Get references from their satisfied clients.

It is wise to be careful when you refer your clients to outside experts. If you are using the services of another professional for the first time, stay involved and walk your clients through the relationship with your new colleague. Then monitor the rela-

How Can You Develop a Network of Professionals?

- Make new contacts at conferences. Do not spend all your time with people who do the same thing you do. Look for people who complement your services.

- Join professional associations. Watch for people with interesting specialties who can become your colleagues. Exchange information about your work and theirs so you can call on each other when it is appropriate.

- Volunteer to serve your professional organizations. You can meet good people who share your concerns but bring different qualifications and training to the table.

- Teach at a local college. Attend faculty meetings and see what the instructors of other courses have to offer.

- Meet people through your colleagues. Ask colleagues to recommend a professional you can call for a particular need. I recently met a skilled international tax expert and renewed ties with a mortgage counselor this way.

- Become active in your local chamber of commerce. There you will find a mix of skills and professions. You may even meet some people who can use your services for their clients.

- Join a business owners' organization. I belong to an organization for female business owners and another for financial specialists. You will share a commonality of interests and meet a wide variety of professionals.

- Ask your friends for introductions. They may have interesting acquaintances you do not know about. Once they know you have a need, they will likely share names of their contacts with you.

tionship and the results. When the work is complete, ask your clients to report back to you on the quality of advice they receive and on the outcome of the relationship. Then you will know whether to refer other clients to the same professional in the future.

Ten Steps to Good Service

Good service for your clients' *financial needs* means providing a quality product or a superior plan in response to a need, presenting it in a timely fashion, implementing it, and monitoring it. Good service for your clients' *human needs* has to do with these 10 components:

1. *Identify the Need.* This is the first step to managing your clients' financial lives. Be alert to what your clients tell you. Look for the crux of the problem.

2. *Anticipate the Need.* In some restaurants, the waiter serves water to your party as soon as you are seated. In other restaurants, you have to ask for water four times before the waiter fills your glasses. The first waiter anticipates your thirst before it occurs; the second does not respond to your need until you bring it up several times. To provide outstanding service, think about your clients' needs and fulfill them before they are aware of them. How? You have done this before. You know what clients will need. Be alert, aware, and act quickly.

3. *Listen Carefully.* Listen to your clients and make sure you hear what is important to them. Question them until you understand what issues are significant. Then respond so clients know you got it. To have a meeting of the minds, say "I hear you" and repeat their message back to them.

4. *Be Available.* Do not make your clients track you down, leave umpteen messages, and find you out of touch. Put your clients first, let them know you are available for them, and prove it by dealing with clients' important issues when they arise.

5. *Respond to the Need.* Let your clients know that you take their problems seriously and that you are searching for the proper solutions. Even before you begin working on the situation, recognize that they have a need, are in a state of uncertainty or discomfort, and let them know that you will help them.

6. *Determine a Course of Action.* Analyze the situation, examine alternatives, and decide on a plan. Think of the steps necessary to implement your plan.

7. *Take Action.* Once you have determined the appropriate action, do it. Do not delay. One planner I know was contacted when his client was on his deathbed. The family wanted to make sure his legal affairs were in order. The planner meant to contact a lawyer but never got around to it. He delayed for a long time, and the client died without drawing up new documents that might have made a difference. If something has to be done, do it as soon as possible.

8. *Fulfill Your Promise.* Devote your time to finding an appropriate solution and fix the problem as much as possible. Doing so will ease your clients' comfort and increase their confidence in your services.

9. *Complete Your Projects.* Do not start a project and drop it when another comes along. Halfway measures will not count to your clients. To make sure you finish each project, use a work status list like mine to let you know what remains to be done (see sidebar "Altfest Client Status List").

10. *Go Beyond.* Do what your clients expect and more. Here are some ideas for separating yourself from the other financial professionals out there. Finish plans earlier than you promised. Implement more items than the client requested, call more often than the client expects, and ask the client back one more time than your agreement calls for. Surprise your clients by going beyond the expected. My favorite client response when I present my work is, "This is so much more than I expected." That really makes my day. Surprise your client in ways that he or she will remember. Make your clients' financial lives a little less stressful. This is client service at its best.

Managing Your Clients' Expectations

One way to provide extra value is to help your clients arrive at realistic expectations for their financial lives and for the work that you do. Help them set practical goals from the moment you

Altfest Client Status List

Client Name_____

Planner in Charge_____

Date Assigned_____

Project	Oral	Written	One-Time Review	Ongoing Client
Financial Plan				
Retirement Plan				
Investment Review				
Investment Management				
Estate Plan				
Other_____				

Status	Date
Engagement Agreement Signed	
Questionnaire Mailed	
Questionnaire Received	
Work Begun	
Figure Input	
Figures Sent Out for Client Review	
Figures Received	
Investments Reviewed	
Asset Allocation Set	
First Draft Written	
First Draft Reviewed by _____	
Revisions Made	
Final Copy Written	
Client Called for Appointment	
Presentation Made	
Additional Work Required	
Follow-Up Set	
Follow-Up Performed	
Project Closed	

Client Billed _____

Client Paid _____

Remarks _____

Note that you can add any items that are helpful and delete any that are irrelevant to your practice. All categories require a date and the initials of the planner next to them, so that anyone who looks at the client's file can have as full information about the status of a project as possible.

The first few items of my status report will look like this when it is completed:

Engagement Agreement Signed	6/19	KA
Questionnaire Mailed	6/19	HC
Questionnaire Received	7/2	PP
Work Begun	7/5	KA

I clip this report to the cover of each client's file folder. By providing complete information, members of my staff can plot the progress of each project and have a chain of responsibility that I can easily access.

take the first call, through meetings in your office, presentation of your work, and for the duration of your ongoing services.

I find it helps clients to be clear on what you are doing for them, how long it will take, what their role is expected to be, and how much you can accomplish for them. To be sure they understand what you are saying, ask your clients if they have questions. Then you can follow up your meetings with a brief summary of what you have discussed.

You can put some items, such as the work you will be doing, in an engagement agreement with your clients. Some other items, however, cannot easily be put into writing. For example, I always tell my clients how long a plan will take, but some of that depends on how quickly my client sends information and documents to me. If I wait six months for the client's tax return, the plan will be delayed. I tell the client that in my first meeting, but few clients who are procrastinators want to assume responsibility for their part in delaying the work.

Recently, I was reminded about the importance of reviewing and managing client expectations. I heard from Rachel, a client who said she was disappointed in her investment account. I checked Rachel's account and found that, in a year in which the stock market had negative returns, her account was up 15 percent. I thought that was a very strong return with a moderate level of risk. Why was Rachel disappointed? Because her head was filled with success stories of the last decade and not with rational projections for the future. This call reinforced what I already know: Tell your clients not once but periodically what they can expect. Ask them many times what they hope to achieve. Try to find out at least annually what concerns clients have and put those in the proper perspective. Let clients know if they are on their way to achieving their goals and what more they have to do.

After all that is said and done, you still have to be on top of your clients' concerns. How can you manage your clients' expectations?

- Disseminate information on a regular basis. Let your clients know what you are doing, why you are doing it, what the project will look like on completion, and how it is appropriate for their needs.

- Have frequent conversations that let you know what your client is thinking. Find out what has changed for the client since your last discussion.

- Tell your clients how they are doing relative to others so they are not in the dark. A 15 percent return is fair sometimes and superior at other times. It is hard for your clients to know which is right at a given time.

- Temper your clients' expectations about investment returns by talking to them about historical rates of return, reminding them that markets fluctuate and even decline, and that good returns generally take a period of time to achieve.

- Do not let clients wonder about anything you are doing for them. If you are behind in a task, do not hope the clients will not notice. Call and explain what is going on.

- Explain your procedures up front. You may think that you work quickly, but if the client has different expectations, you will be the loser.

- Show your clients that you are sensitive to their concerns. I always ask clients if there is something they need done in a special hurry. Then, if the full job takes some time, I can get the time-sensitive part of the job done first.

Communicate, Communicate, Communicate

One of the most important lessons that I have learned from 15 years in the financial services business is to invest the time and effort to communicate often, clearly, and simply with my clients. I believe that this is the big lesson that can help you achieve your goals for building your business and retaining clients for life. Whether you seek fame and fortune or simply desire a stable practice and a solid client base, this should be your golden rule of client service: Communicate clearly, regularly, and consistently with your clients. Setting up an easy, comfortable, nonthreatening relationship in which your client hears from you often and is free to tell you anything is so important that I have said it three times so that you will not forget it.

No matter how developed your communication skills are, you are in luck. There are many ways to communicate with your clients. You do not have to practice all of them, or any of them all the time. You can pick and choose the ones that fit your style. If you are better at writing than speaking, there are some ideas that will work for you. If you prefer communicating electronically, you will find some easy and quick ways to maintain contact. If you like one-on-one meetings, you can arrange in-person conferences. Adopt the ways of communication that suit your practice and your personality, change them whenever you find they no longer work, and think of proprietary ways to set you apart from your colleagues.

Once you get used to communicating regularly with your clients, you will soon find that it is simple and fun to think up new methods of getting your word out and meeting the needs of your client base. You can experiment with in-house printing, try your hand at graphics, and let your creative side shine. You can capture the attention of prospects and clients in your community. In this twenty-first century, I believe the financial professionals who put time and effort into becoming effective communicators will have a leg up when it comes to keeping clients for life.

Eleven Ways to Communicate with Your Clients

Following are 11 ways to communicate with your clients. Choose those that you are comfortable with and adapt them to your unique style. Feel free to discard the rest, and to create new methods yourself.

1. *Phone Calls.* Telephoning is a very direct way of reaching out to your clients. Find a time when you are not rushed, think of a worthwhile reason to call, and let your voice express your pleasure and interest in speaking to each client. Reasons to call may include asking how things are going or bringing the client up-to-date on some relevant news. Think of your reason before you dial the client's number.

2. *Letters.* I try to send something to my clients each month. It could be a newspaper clipping on a topic we have been discussing, a personal letter, or my year-end letter that I send out each December in lieu of a holiday card.

3. *E-Mail.* I have two e-mail addresses. I get so much mail that I try to download it a few times each day. It has become apparent that many of my clients prefer to be in touch electronically, maybe because it reduces the need for social niceties. It is quick and easy to dash off a few lines to a client on a topic of interest. Be sure to keep a hard copy of all correspondence for your files.

4. *Web Site.* Consider investing in a Web site as a good way to let prospects and clients know what you are thinking and to access their accounts even when you are not in the office. Make sure your site represents you and your style. Make it attractive, easy to use, clear, and helpful.

5. *Newsletter.* My firm has two newsletters. One we buy from a financial writer, add a cover article, and send to our clients. My staff creates the other one based on issues that interest us and our clients at the time. It is hard to find the time to do our own newsletter, but it reflects our values and our philosophy very clearly. My staff's newsletter is my favorite because it reflects the current thinking at my firm. It keeps our name in front of clients, and gets them think-

Sample Year-End Letter

Dear Client,

As the year draws to a close, we want to share some recent events at L.J. Altfest & Co., Inc. with you. We have been particularly busy this year. We have updated our hardware and software systems, added a new database, and simplified our quarterly reports. We are confident that everything is in place for a smooth passage to the New Year.

We have added to our staff so that we can provide better service to you. For a list of our employees and the functions they serve, please consult our Web site at www.altfest.com. Speaking of our Web site, we now have a link through which you can access your account directly via the Internet. We recently sent you a letter explaining how to do this.

The seminar programs we presented to you have been very well received. This year we invited a mutual fund manager to speak to you, invited clients to our seminars at the New School, and brought an estate attorney to speak to clients with concerns about passing assets to the next generation. Our own professional staff spoke about reducing your debt, total return, and how to read your financial statement. We are designing an exciting program for you and your guests for the coming year.

We are looking forward to the New Year. We value you as a client, and are interested in helping you reach your personal goals. We hope that in the coming year we will see you often and spend even more time helping you with your financial needs.

We wish you and your family a healthy and productive year ahead and a happy holiday season!

Sincere regards,

ing about important issues. It is time-consuming to produce, but well worth the effort. And who says it has to look like the *Wall Street Journal?* Keep it brief, and send yours out each month or every quarter.

6. *Seminars.* My husband and I each give many seminars at local universities, libraries, and organizations. We both like to teach and enjoy feedback from the audience. We invite existing clients and their friends to seminars that would interest them. Generally, many of our clients attend. Our

client Frank jokes that he comes to sit in the front row and heckle us. Like Frank, our clients tend to keep us on our toes.

7. *Quarterly Reports.* This is an important part of my firm's communications with our investment management clients and a very good way to stay in touch. It concerns something that is generally of great interest to our clients—their portfolios. What you say in your report and how you say it will help determine what your clients think of you. Avoid the temptation to use jargon. Use appropriate benchmarks to measure your performance, and remember to include an easy-to-understand narrative along with your numbers.

8. *Birthday and Anniversary Cards.* I know many advisors who send out cards for every occasion. One colleague of mine got things backwards and for years sent me a birthday card on my husband's birthday and sent my husband a card on mine. If you plan to send cards, take care to get the information right. Personally, I would not care to get birthday cards from my attorney or accountant, so I send cards to my clients only on very special occasions: births, adoptions, deaths, marriages, illnesses, special birthdays, and major anniversaries. Clients like to be remembered. Do what feels comfortable for your practice.

9. *Dinners.* Some planners invite their most substantial clients and those who refer new business to them to dinner. My clients are so busy, I do not think that works well. Four years ago when our firm moved to new quarters, we had a large reception for clients. I am thinking of having another one next year when my firm will celebrate its 20th anniversary. For now, I supply refreshments at office events, offer lunch or dinner to people who have traveled a long way, and leave it at that.

10. *Outings.* My colleagues around the country tell me they have successfully orchestrated golf trips, boat rides, as well as movies for clients' children. I love parties, but feel uncomfortable planning my clients' weekends. Do it if other professionals in your city tell you it works.

11. *Postcards.* When I am involved in special events, such as seminars that might interest my clients, I send out a postcard that notifies clients of the time, date, place, and topic of the event. I invite my clients to come as my guests, even if there is a fee involved for other attendees. Sometimes, I even pay their entrance fee myself. I always ask clients to respond to my office so that I will know who and how many are attending. Since there is no formal registration, accepting with a phone call to your office commits your clients to attend the event. As an extra precaution, send out a brief reminder a few days before the event.

Postcard Invitation

L.J. Altfest & Co., Inc. is pleased to invite you and a guest to Lew Altfest's seminar "How to Read the *Wall Street Journal*"

When: Monday, January 21
             6–8 P.M.

Where: The New School
            66 West 12th Street
            New York City

RSVP: Call Helen at 212-xxx-xxxx

Experience Counts

Whether you are on your own or at an established business, to get ahead you have to develop your financial skills, business skills, service skills, and people skills. Education and training in the financial field is a given. Service is what can distinguish you from your peers. Even if you have all the necessary characteristics, there are people who will not take you seriously if you are perceived as too young, too inexperienced, or in the business for too short a period.

It takes time to build up your skills, develop a practice, and convince people you know what you are doing. Learning to deliver good service takes both time and experience. First, all aspects of your business have to be stable to allow you to be a good service provider. Yet patience can be difficult. What can you do to jump-start the process?

- *Get Experience.* Get your feet wet in someone else's office. Learn the ropes and write a business plan before moving into your own business.

- *Use Your Contacts.* Draw on your personal and business acquaintances to help you get started. Even if you have transitioned from another career, think of people you know who can offer you advice and contacts.

- *Pay Your Dues.* Offer pro bono help to not-for-profit organizations, the elderly, and others who need it. Show that you care about your local community, build your experience, and keep your name in circulation.

- *Do Not Fight the Demographics.* Work with people like you. If you are starting at a young age, think of all those people in their twenties and thirties who would not feel comfortable with an advisor who reminds them of their aunt or uncle and offer your services to them. If you are nearing retirement age, specialize in clients who are retired and would not want to work with someone who is the age of their grandchildren.

- *Do Not Bury Your Past.* If you were a dentist in a previous career, do not turn your back on your fellow dentists who need your help. Contact dental societies and offer financial planning for professionals whom you truly understand.

- *Do Not Rush Things.* Expect that it may take time to convince people that you have the credentials and experience necessary to be a legitimate, credible advisor. Sow seeds now that can blossom at different points of time. Join organizations, get speaking engagements, take on small clients, and build on your name, your growing expertise, and your expanding skills.

- *Network.* Meet colleagues through professional organizations. Form alliances with those at your level and learn from those who have been around longer than you. Make yourself available to take on the work they do not have time for. I have helped many people start their practices by referring clients who do not fit my firm's profile. Find some professionals who can do the same for you.

- *Earn a Reputation for Delivering Service.* Once you have all the mechanisms in place for running an efficient business, you can focus on how to provide outstanding service. If you do not deliver good service to your clients, you will not be on anybody's growth and referral list. Go the extra step, give your clients what they ask for, and what they did not know they needed. Treat referrals from clients, colleagues, and friends with extra care so that many more will follow.

Schmoozing

Although they do not teach this in business school, schmoozing can be a great way to let your clients know you are thinking about them and their financial circumstances. If you enjoy making small talk with clients, you have a great business skill. Work on it, play it up, and integrate small talk into the beginning of all conversations with your clients. If you are not a natural schmoozer, you can show that you are thinking of your clients in other ways.

Since I cannot always see my clients as often as I would like, at my firm I let the three c's—calling cards, calls, and conversation— be my guide.

Calling Cards. In Victorian times, people visited each other's houses and left a calling card to say that they had been there. Meeting someone in person was nice, but letting them know you thought of them and stopped by could be even more important socially. Let your clients know you are thinking of them by sending your calling card. Decide on a card that represents you and get a large supply. I use simple, elegant stationery from a local museum to send out personal notes to clients, colleagues, and prospects. I believe my notes show I am remembering them in a special way. The bonus is that it takes only a few minutes to dash off a note.

Calls. Although I do not hook myself up to a headset, sometimes I do feel permanently attached to the phone at my ear.

I make calls for many occasions: to share news, ask about family matters, or just to alert the client that I will be sending some material out and to watch for it. The bonus is that very often I come away with more information about my client's circumstances than I had when I lifted the receiver.

Conversation. If you are weak at spontaneous conversation but want to give schmoozing a try, note the four types of conversation:

1. *Acceptable but Dull.* This category includes weather and traffic. Try for something acceptable, more personal, and less dull. My husband Lew always asks new prospects if they had trouble finding our office. There is no right or wrong answer, but the question gives people a chance to tell us something safe about themselves and reduces the tension in the first meeting.

2. *Unacceptable but Dull.* If you think a topic is unacceptable, stay away. No one wants to hear you complain about your staff, your health, or your family. Being confrontational, critical, or telling off-color jokes will not bring you closer to your clients. Talk about topics that will not offend anyone.

3. *Unacceptable but Interesting.* Stories about others and giving away confidences are included in this category. It is unacceptable to tell shocking stories about clients even if you do not divulge their names. This is a sure trust destroyer. Do not go there.

4. *Acceptable and Interesting.* These are the topics you should search for. Economic news, stories about hobbies (either yours or theirs), tales of recent trips, and news of great sporting or entertainment events all qualify just as they would over dinner with friends. If you can find topics that genuinely interest both you and your clients and establish a common bond, you are exhibiting top schmoozing form.

Determine whether you are a better storyteller or listener and assume that role in your conversations. If you are better at listening, let the client direct the small talk. If you are a great storyteller, go ahead, share your tales, but come up for air often enough so your client can participate in the conversation. Most important, get into your client's world. Find out individual interests and schmooze about them. Following is a sample conversation:

Planner: Hi, Dave. Hi, Marie. It's good to see you. You're both looking relaxed. Are you having a good summer?

Dave: Yes, it's been great. We were at the beach for two weeks.

Planner: Did you have good weather?

Marie: It rained for the first three days, and then it cleared up.

Planner: *(Empathizing)* That's lucky. You must have enjoyed being there.

Marie: Yes. We swam, and barbecued, and visited our friends.

Planner: *(Personalizing)* I've always liked the beach. Did you stay at a hotel or rent a cottage?

Marie: No. My cousin owns a cabin at the beach and he wasn't using it, so he invited us to stay there.

Planner: How nice. It's wonderful to get away, have time to yourselves, and come back refreshed.

Dave: I know. Now we're revitalized and ready to return to work.

Planner: *(Taking the cue)* That's good. Come into my office and let's get started.

While this brief, casual conversation seems to be about nothing much, do not be fooled. It is about establishing ties with your clients, making a connection, showing your interest in their lives, and getting to know them and their lifestyles better. It is a way of understanding their needs and fitting your service to their situations. The rapport you develop in small doses over time can lead to better relationships, greater trust, and genuine feelings of warmth toward you, the advisor your clients want to keep for life.

Be There for Your Clients

Ultimately, good service is the value you add in your relationship with your clients. It is anything you do with your clients' best interests in mind. True service is not peripheral to the planning process, but a major component. Establishing and maintaining a comfortable, respectful and mutually satisfying relationship with your clients allows the financial work to proceed smoothly and your association to continue over a long period of time. It is how you differentiate your firm from others and how you stand out in a crowded field of advisors.

Recently, I had lunch with Rich, an advisor who specializes in high–net-worth individuals who have $10 million or more in investable assets. Rich handles his clients' portfolios, negotiates leases for them, pays their bills, and does their accounting from his office or their homes. When I asked Rich exactly what he does for his clients, he replied, "Anything they want me to do." Rich has made himself valuable to wealthy individuals by being there for them. While he is not irreplaceable, Rich's clients count on him to coordinate the various financial parts of their lives.

I believe my clients deserve the same level of service and so do yours. While I do not usually travel to my clients' homes, and I do not pay their bills, I do stay on top of developments in their busy lives and coordinate many aspects of their financial circumstances. I am willing to set aside other projects to help a client in distress. Most of all, I want to make sure my clients are on solid financial footing, and I will do what it takes to get them there.

Like Rich, you can be the kind of planner clients lean on. You can supply that extra service that binds your clients to you. Let clients know you welcome their questions and their calls and that you are available to serve them whenever they need you. As word gets out that you offer superior service, your clients will feel satisfied, your referrals will increase, you will find yourself in demand, and you will keep many clients for life.

CHAPTER

11

Three Ways to Rate Yourself

Number One: Surveys

Whether you are a new planner or an experienced one, with many clients or only a few, in a small or large firm, it is important for the growth and success of your business and the happiness of your clients to take time at least once a year to get feedback about your performance and services.

I believe surveys are the best way to get client input, to learn about the needs and wants of your clients, and to adjust your services to meet those needs. If you do not take the time to ask about your clients' thoughts and feelings, you might get no information from unhappy clients until an emergency develops.

You can interview your clients in the four following ways:

1. In person

2. On the telephone

3. In focus groups

4. By means of a written or oral questionnaire

If you interview your clients in person, you have the benefit of observing their reactions to your questions. You can gear additional questions to clients' responses as you proceed. But you have the disadvantage of putting clients on the spot, making them uncomfortable, and taking the risk that your clients will say only nice things to please you. I suspect this is the least likely method of gaining truthful, spontaneous answers.

If you schedule telephone interviews, you can hire a consultant to interview your clients. I engaged Dr. F., a psychologist, to telephone my clients. Dr. F. managed to be understanding and discreet, yet thorough. Because Dr. F. could call on behalf of my company yet say that he was an independent consultant who would not reveal anything the client wanted to keep confidential, I believe he was able to gain more information than I would have received had I made the calls. I think telephone surveys work very well. Unlike written surveys, they allow spontaneous follow-up to your initial questions. Since the interviewer and the respondent are not in the same room, telephone interviews permit a measure of anonymity, which may encourage some clients to answer more freely.

Following is a sample phone interview with a long-term client:

Interviewer:	Hello, Mrs. Hastings. I am calling on behalf of L.J. Altfest & Co., Inc. I am an independent consultant the company has engaged to find out what their clients like about working with them and what suggestions clients like you have for change. Is this a good time for you to talk?
Client:	I have some time. How long will this take?
Interviewer:	Our conversation should take about 15 minutes.
Client:	That's fine.
Interviewer:	Great. Let's get started. *(To get the client comfortable, the interviewer starts with simple factual questions.)* How long have you been a client of the firm?
Client:	About five years.
Interviewer:	What kind of work does L.J. Altfest do for you?
Client:	They manage my portfolio and advise me on saving money for my retirement.

Interviewer: *(Encouragingly)* Good. When is the last time you met with your advisors?

Client: I was there about two months ago.

From these factual background questions, the interviewer can now switch to questions that require the client to form an opinion about the firm. The interviewer will spend more or less time on each question depending on the client's involvement and the firm's need to gain information in a particular area.

Interviewer: Do you generally see the same advisor?

Client: Yes, I usually see Paul.

Interviewer: How do you feel about your meetings with Paul?

If the client is at a loss for comment, the interviewer can be more specific about the quality of the relationship (Does Paul spend too much time, not enough time, or just the right amount of time with you?), the work done (Was the work satisfactory or unsatisfactory?), and expectations surpassed or unmet (Do you feel the work done met your needs, surpassed your needs, or did not meet your needs?). Before the interview ends, the consultant will ask about the physical setting of the office, timeliness of work done, promises delivered, any disappointments, general overall satisfaction with the relationship, and additional services that the client would like access to.

If you use a professional interviewer, she can spot trends and delve more deeply into them with clients. For example, if many people are disappointed in a certain area, the interviewer can ask targeted questions that will help determine the cause.

If professional interviewers are not in your budget, you can train staff members to conduct interviews. Note that you should begin with a training session on interview techniques and what you hope to accomplish. Tell your staff that it is important not to put answers in clients' mouths, to listen to a complete response without interrupting, and to ask some open-ended questions that can lead to more information than anticipated.

You can also survey your clients in a focus group. Typically, the company paying for the focus group offers the clients something in return for participating, such as a dinner, cash payment, or a nonmonetary reward. Groups typically meet for two hours. Ideally, focus groups should not be held at your premises in order to keep the transaction at arm's length and not make the client feel responsible to you. Since it is important to elicit useful information and avoid irrelevant discussions, you should choose a trained professional interviewer to lead the group. A good leader will work with you to learn the kinds of information that would benefit your company and to structure questions, discussions, and exercises that will elicit that information.

Finally, you can mail a written survey to your clients or post one on your Internet site. Unlike the follow-up questionnaire that deals with a specific project, these surveys elicit information about your firm overall. Although written surveys allow you to reach out to the greatest number of clients, this is the least personal approach and will probably gain the lowest rate of answers. Written questionnaires are not much different from other surveys, but the human interaction is missing. Since clients cannot receive clarification of the questions, you may encounter incomplete answers and misunderstood directions. Questions are simply as stated and cannot be developed further.

No matter how you deliver your questions, do not make your surveys too long. Limit yourself to just a few topics, and no more than 2 to 4 pages, or 15 to 20 minutes on the phone. Determine what would be most helpful to know about your clients' lives, your relationships with them, and their opinions about your business practices. Take the time to compose the right questions. If you hire consultants, ask for their help in directing the questions so that you can learn to improve professional and client service. Divide your questions into sections that you want to know about. Use these criteria as a guide to get the information you want on the topics you wish to learn about:

Office:
1. The appearance of your office
2. The location of your office
3. The convenience of your hours
4. The ease of scheduling appointments

Professionalism:
5. Your professional knowledge
6. Your understanding of clients' issues

7. Your products

8. Your presentation

Service: 9. Timeliness of getting advice

10. Communication skills

11. Client's comfort level while working with you

12. How well the advisor (you) understood client's concerns

Staff Members: 13. Staff competency

14. Staff geniality

15. Responsiveness and availability of staff

16. Helpfulness of staff

Value: 17. Usefulness of advice rendered

18. Has client implemented advisor's suggestions

19. Was client able to ask all his or her questions of the advisor

20. Was client able to come back for follow-up sessions as needed

When you prepare your survey, add any topics that interest you, delete those that are of no interest, and expand on others that are of particular concern. Always have one or two general questions, such as, "Are there any other services you would like us to offer?" or, "Is there anything else you want us to know?" Clients should be able to offer feedback on anything that catches their attention, and not be restricted by your list.

In my experience, in all modes of questioning your clients have a better rate of return and fuller results if the interviewer is well prepared. Be clear, avoid questions that are biased toward the answer you desire, and make sure each question asks only about one item. For example, if you ask clients if they are pleased with the promptness and follow-up at your firm, they may be pleased with the promptness and displeased with the follow-up, but can give only one answer. Separate those items into two

Here is a questionnaire I use in my firm as one of several ways we elicit client feedback. You should modify it to meet your needs.

Client Service Questionnaire

In order to improve our services, we would like feedback from our clients. The questions should not take very long to answer. If you wish, your comments will remain anonymous.

1. What was the nature of the service(s) rendered for you?
2. Discuss and rate the service from 5 (highest) to 1 (lowest) based on the following criteria:
   a. Ease in understanding the work done
   b. Results relative to what you wanted
   c. Promptness
   d. Fees
   e. Did you receive value
   f. Communication with staff members
   g. Staff helpfulness
   h. Continuing relationship
   i. Materials received from firm
3. What are the strengths of the company?
4. What are the weaknesses of the company?
5. Is there anything you wanted done that was *not done* for you?
6. What is your appraisal of the firm overall?
7. Do you have any suggestions for improving our services?
8. Are there additional services you could use?
9. Would you refer friends or colleagues to L.J. Altfest & Co., Inc.? If not, why?
10. If yes to No. 9, are there any people you would like us to send literature to?

Great! You have completed our client service questionnaire.

Thank you for your help!

Your name (optional): _____

questions. Now that you have decided what you want to include, prepare a survey that covers your main topics.

I always drop a note to my clients a week before I send out a survey or before I allow a consultant to call. I alert clients that the survey is coming, and explain why it is important to us to have their opinions on a number of topics. I believe preparing clients in advance puts them in a better frame of mind, makes them feel less imposed upon, and results in a better rate of return.

Sample Client Survey Alert

Dear Mr. and Mrs. Client,

We are interested in learning what you think about our financial services and our relationship with you. Therefore, we have composed a brief survey, which we will be mailing out one week from today.

Please take the time to share your thoughts. The survey should take no longer than 20 minutes to complete.

We value your opinions and look forward to seeing your responses.

Sincerely,

To get a greater response, enclose a self-addressed, stamped envelope. You can also consider including an incentive with your mailing, such as a book you think will appeal to most clients. Some companies send crisp new dollar bills with a survey. That seems to work even with individuals who are not clients of the company. Other companies offer to contribute a small sum to charity for every survey that is completed. For people I know, I prefer a personal gift or none at all.

If responses are slow in arriving, send out postcards reminding clients that they received your survey and telling them how important it is to you to have their opinions. Give them a number to call if they have misplaced their surveys. Tell them the deadline for returning their responses.

Once you receive your clients' feedback, it is up to you to read, tally, interpret, and react to the results. Assign numerical values to each possible answer and determine the frequency of responses. Look for patterns and areas of dissatisfaction. Then decide how you will respond to this information. If you hear that your clients do not like the location of your office, are you going to move? If not, perhaps there are steps you can take to keep your clients happy and show them you are paying attention to their comments. Consider hiring a car service to bring clients to you, or prepaying a parking garage near your office to encourage clients to drive to your office. Join a club in a more accessible part of town and hold meetings there, perhaps over lunch.

What are some things I have learned from client surveys over the years? One client, Sammy, wrote that he came to our firm because he heard we specialize in women, retirees, professors, and physicians. Although Sammy was none of these, he thought it sounded nice and wanted to be included. That indicated to me that Sammy was looking for a caring atmosphere and people who enjoy lively discussion, as doctors and professors are likely to do. Another client, Rick, told me he came to our roundtable seminars partly to hear the speakers and partly because he liked the food we served. I believe Rick is searching for extra comfort and nurturing. But none stands out in my memory more than Rhoda, who told my consultant she considers my office her home away from home. What a nice thing to say!

Of course, there has been constructive criticism over the years as well, and we have responded promptly to it. Like me, I suggest you share knowledge of your findings with your staff. Discuss the information you have gathered with your colleagues and determine what action you will take. Keep an open mind about the results and do not take client criticism personally. Think in terms of what you can do to improve your products and services. If many clients think your fees are too high, adjust your fees, add more service for the same prices, or look for a new client base. If clients say they will not refer their friends to you, make yours a firm that people will want to bring their friends to. Find out what your clients object to, and make appropriate changes. Send out a letter to all your clients detailing the changes in your firm. Let clients know how much you appreciate their suggestions and how responsive you are to them.

Do not bury your head in the sand and accuse clients of not knowing what they are talking about. Having an outside consultant can keep the findings on a professional level and help you maintain your objectivity about the results. Most people know what they like. Feel privileged to be given this valuable information. Take action to improve your relationships with your clients.

Number Two: Client Retention

Reviewing how many of your clients you are keeping for life is one indication of how you are doing in delivering your services. No matter what clients tell you, they will talk most clearly with their feet. If you are experiencing mass migrations, consider hiring someone to call those clients who leave and ask why they changed advisors. You can construct an exit survey that will zero in on client complaints, unfulfilled expectations, and reasons for leaving. Some clients leave because they are afraid they are missing something elsewhere; others may have tangible complaints or comments about your services. Listen carefully to what they tell you. Then it is up to you to make the necessary adjustments in your practice.

The dream for many advisors is to retain 100 percent of their clients. Since clients die, divorce, relocate, and experience other major life changes, it is impossible to retain everyone. However, if your turnover exceeds 10 percent per year, take a good look at your practices and procedures and uncover what improvements you can make. If you are losing more than 20 percent of your client base each year, you may have to conduct some emergency management to stop the losses, while you figure out the underlying problems at your firm. Emergency management can include the following steps:

- Call all clients. Remember your clients like to hear from you, and this gives you the opportunity to know what they are thinking as well as tell them what improvements you are making.

- Notify your clients of changes in your practices. If there are problems, let clients know you are aware of them and working to eradicate them.

- Review all portfolios and identify weak spots. If clients have unrealistic expectations, you can talk to them and set realistic goals.

- Add a client service representative to your practice. This provides an opportunity to share the calls and let clients voice complaints to someone else if they are reluctant to talk to you personally. It also allows your firm to focus extra attention on certain clients.

- Schedule more frequent client meetings. Even clients who do not have much time appreciate that you are thinking of them and their needs. They may agree to set aside a few hours to meet with you when you point out how it can benefit them.

- Review the practices of all employees, identify trouble spots, and act promptly to correct them. Make sure everyone in your firm puts the clients first and that your clients know this.

Note that if you are losing more clients than you add each year, something may be seriously wrong with your client service or professional practices. You may want to hire a business consultant to review your operations, staff, systems, services, and other practices. If hiring a professional is out of the question, consider asking a respected colleague or other advisor to review your methods of operation. You can also form a committee of business advisors, clients, and colleagues to serve as an advisory council to your business.

Another indication of how you compare in the universe of financial advisors is how often clients refer their friends and families to you. This will not be a totally accurate measurement because many satisfied clients prefer not to share their favored advisors. However, if you have a very low level of referrals, you can search for reasons. Have you created a practice that you would bring your own friends and relatives to?

Each year, create a chart that tells you how many clients you have, how long they have been with you, and what new clients they have referred to you within the last 12 months. Your client referral chart can look like this:

Client Referral Chart

Client	Inception Date	Referrals Last 12 Months
R. Brown	1988	2
A. Stevens	1994	0
P. Miller	2001	1
J. Estabrook	1999	4

You should also create a chart for clients who leave, giving the inception date, when they left, and the reason for leaving if known. Your client departure chart can look like this:

Client Departure Chart

Client	Inception Date	Date Left	Reason
E. Diamond	1996	2001	Illness
B. Freeman	1982	2002	Divorce
C. Bernstein	1999	2001	Relocation

To have a good idea of where you stand, keep accurate records. Compare your turnover each year with other years. Study your departure chart and find out what steps you can take to keep this list from growing. Look for trends in any one reason over time. The great majority of reasons for leaving should have to do with life's transitions, not with your services. Keep on the lookout to make sure this is true with your client base.

Number Three: Your Satisfaction

The third way to rate yourself is to stop what you are doing, take a close look at all phases of your operation, and decide if you are satisfied with what you have accomplished. This may be the first time you have thought about using yourself as a performance measure. Here is an opportunity for you to review your systems, setting, operations, personnel, client base, plans and products, and follow-up, and determine if it is all you want it to be. Create a checklist to help you examine each area. Here are some factors I look for in each area when I review my business:

Systems:	Do they make use of current technology?
	Are they efficient?
	Are they up-to-date?
	Do they produce accurate results?
	Are they cost-effective?
	Have I heard of others that are better or broader in their capabilities?
Setting:	Is my work environment convenient?
	Is it attractive?
	Is it calm?
	Is it comfortable for clients?
	Is it easy to maintain?
	Does it look professional?
Operations:	Are my firm's operations modern?
	Are they well organized?
	Are they efficient?
	Are they cost-effective?
	Are they easy to run and maintain?
	Do they allow me to deliver work promptly?
Personnel:	Are my employees highly skilled?
	Are they personable?
	Are they competent?
	Are they efficient?
	Is their demeanor business-like?
	Are they up-to-date on modern business techniques?

Clients: Do my clients have problems I can help solve?

Do they have the level of assets and income that I want to work with?

Do they have educations and job situations that I am comfortable with?

Is this a good fit for the clients and for me?

Are my clients satisfied with the work I do for them?

Are most of my relationships long-lasting and ongoing?

Financial Plans and Products: Do my plans represent the level of knowledge and expertise I have?

Are my plans simple and clear?

Are they presented attractively and professionally?

Am I proud to deliver them?

Do products meet my clients' needs?

Is there anything more I could offer?

Follow-Up: Do I clearly tell clients what I expect them to do?

Do I contact clients frequently to check on their progress?

Am I available for clients' questions and problems?

Do my staff members follow up regularly with clients?

Do we make it comfortable for clients to seek our help?

Are we satisfied with our follow-up procedures?

Assess those areas that represent your unique skills, characteristics, and qualities. Think about what you hope to accomplish and make sure you are on target. Your list should reflect you, what you do well, and your particular client base, just as mine reflects me and my business.

After compiling your list, compliment yourself on what you do well and make adjustments to items you can improve. I spend more waking time in my business than in my home. I like to believe it is all worthwhile, that I bring value and concrete results to my clients. Make sure you are satisfied with all areas of your professional life if you wish to satisfy your clients.

Once you have implemented all three ways of rating yourself—you have sent out or conducted interviews based on your surveys, checked your rate of client retention and determined reasons for departures, and decided whether you are satisfied with your business—there is still one more rating method. Use the Altfest service indicator to determine how you rank.

Circle the procedures you practice regularly and give yourself the points you deserve. Then add them all up to determine your standing.

The Altfest Service Indicator

	Points		
Your Business Practices	*Always*	*Sometimes*	*Rarely*
1. Create a comfortable, relaxed office setting	5	3	0
2. Have a credibility wall	5	3	0
3. Offer in-office refreshments	5	3	0
4. Call clients once a month	5	3	0
5. Send out quarterly reports	5	3	0
6. Have editor review plans annually	5	3	0
7. Create plans that allow for many learning styles	5	3	0
8. Send out professional newsletter each quarter	5	3	0

9. Send out your own newsletter each quarter	5	3	0
10. Create a client survey each year	5	3	0
11. Create a year-end letter	5	3	0
12. Send special occasion cards and calling cards	5	3	0
13. Offer educational experiences for clients	5	3	0
14. Return client calls within 24 hours	5	3	0
15. Complete client work promptly	5	3	0
16. Develop a network of professionals	5	3	0
17. Develop a relationship with members of the media	5	3	0
18. Check on what clients have implemented	5	3	0
19. Invite clients to follow-up sessions	5	3	0
20. Communicate, communicate, communicate	5	3	0

Now score yourself. Celebrate the 5's, improve on the 3's, and beware of those 0's. If you have too many circles in that column, you may watch your clients walk out the door. Set targets and start to improve your areas of weakness. Add up your numbers. If your score is below 70, work on your professional, business, personal, and people skills. If your score is between 70 and 90, you are almost where you want to be.

Take the time to revise your business practices and bring them up to the next level. If you have a score of 90 or above, congratulations! You have what it takes. You are a financial professional who is poised to keep your clients for life!

Appendix

Financial Questionnaire*

Personal Financial Information for

_____

(name)

_____

(date)

In order to facilitate our understanding of your financial affairs, please take some time to complete the following pages. First, you are requested to fill out some basic personal information. Next, you are asked to discuss your financial objectives and goals, an extremely important part of the questionnaire—please give it some serious attention. You are further asked some questions concerning your risk tolerance and investment preferences. Last, you are asked to list your assets, liabilities, income, and expenses. You may use estimates, if necessary, and round to the nearest $100. Please type or clearly print all information you provide.

Please submit the following documents:

_____   Last two years' federal, state, and city tax returns

_____   Estate tax return

_____   Latest statements from money market and mutual funds, brokerage accounts, pension plans, Keogh and IRA accounts, or any other material investments

_____   Insurance policies

_____   Wills and trusts

_____   Mortgage(s), end-of-year statement(s)

_____   Divorce or separation agreement, if applicable

*Reprinted with permission from Mary Malgoire and David Drucker.

_____   Business documents, if applicable

_____   Recent payroll check stub

Please note that your plan will be more precise and timely if we receive as complete and accurate information as possible from you. Information that seems unimportant to you may be of more consequence than you think. Thus, please take time and care to review the information we request. Look over the entire questionnaire before you begin so that you can anticipate all the questions, taking care not to enter the same information in two different sections. Taking a few more hours now will give us the material we need to offer as complete advice as possible.

Personal Information

	Client I	Client II
Name	_____	_____
Sex	_____	_____
Home address	_____	_____
	_____	_____
Home phone	_____	_____
Business address	_____	_____
Business phone	_____	_____
Occupation	_____	_____
How long?	_____	_____
Birth date	_____	_____
Social Security #	_____	_____
Attorney	_____	_____
Phone number	_____	_____
Accountant	_____	_____
Phone number	_____	_____
Broker	_____	_____
Other advisors	_____	_____

| | | | Estimate in Today's Dollars | |
| | | Sending to | College | Room & |
Dependent Children: Name	Age	College	Tuition	Board
_____	____	____	____	____
_____	____	____	____	____
_____	____	____	____	____
_____	____	____	____	____

Self-Supporting Children:

_____	____	____	____	____
_____	____	____	____	____
_____	____	____	____	____
_____	____	____	____	____

Parents: Name	Age	Annual Support Provided
_____	____	____
_____	____	____
_____	____	____
_____	____	____

Are all family members in good health? Explain:

_____

Are any persons dependent on you for support other than your family?

_____

Do you have any alimony or child support obligations?

_____

Other personal information you feel would be relevant to our planning process:

_____

_____

_____

_____

_____

_____

_____

_____

If you are over age 70 and ½, when did you last take an IRA distribution?
_____ Amount _____

Personal Financial Goals and Objectives

Financial goals are sometimes hard to articulate. Objectives such as faster asset growth, paying lower taxes, and protecting assets against inflation are common concerns of most individuals. These are not only financial goals. They also impact your current and future lifestyle. How do you imagine your finances over the next several years? What do you expect your retirement lifestyle to be like? Review your specific situation—current lifestyle considerations, family needs, feelings about risk and investments, alternative career and life plans, health, desired gifts or inheritances to family members, heirs, etc.—and try to review your goals.

This is only a start. We will help you further define and clarify your goals and their financial implications. Please use the next few pages to comment on your goals, their relative priorities to each other, when you hope to reach these goals, and their cost in today's dollars. You may want to have a discussion, take some notes, or reflect before you begin this section. Although we do not expect you to plan your entire future, knowledge of your hopes and expectations can help us work toward a scenario that is appropriate and comfortable for you. Feel free to use additional pages if you need more space.

Client I's goals:

Client II's goals:

We now ask you to quantify some of your goals by responding to the following questions:

Retirement Goals:

At what age do you plan to retire?

Client I: _____

Client II:_____

Number of years you have worked under the Social Security system?

Client I: _____

Client II:_____

Average earnings during these years?

Client I: _____

Client II:_____

Desired after-tax retirement income estimated in today's dollars?

_____

Would you consider moving to a smaller home/condo or relocating after retirement?

_____

Do you have health coverage that will continue after retirement?

Client I: _____

Client II:_____

Do you or your spouse have any conditions or possible burdens that might affect or limit your retirement lifestyle?

_____

_____

Any other concerns or questions about retirement?

_____

_____

Please rank the relative importance of the following goals by number 1 (most important) to 6 (least important):

Improving current standard of living   _____

Comfortable retirement   _____

Building/providing estate for heirs   _____

Educating children   _____

Other: _____   _____

Other: _____   _____

What would you consider your primary financial goal or concern?

_____

_____

To estimate your personal tolerances for risk and investment experience, we ask that you complete the optional following section. If you feel uncomfortable or lack knowledge in the field of investments, please note this below:

Do you have any preferences or objections to any particular investment areas? Do you have any anxieties about investing in general? Please explain:

_____

_____

_____

Please give examples of investments you believe are:

Client I   *Client II*

1. Very Conservative

_____   _____

_____   _____

2. Conservative

_____   _____

_____   _____

3. Moderate Risk

_____   _____

_____   _____

4. High Risk

_____   _____

_____   _____

Using the types of investments you selected in the previous section as a guide for each category, fill out the categories below. In other words, how would you best position your investments to coincide with your investment temperament:

	Client I	Client II
1. Very conservatively (Conserving present capital is critical)	_____%	_____%
2. Conservatively (Some growth desirable)	_____%	_____%
3. Subject to moderate risk (Growth is more important than capital preservation)	_____%	_____%
4. Subject to high risk (Speculative growth is acceptable or desirable)	_____%	_____%

Please assign a numerical rating from 0 to 100 as to how important the following factors are in making investment decisions for the average asset that you hold:

	Client I	Client II
Hedge against inflation	_____	_____
Above-average growth in capital	_____	_____
Stability of principal	_____	_____
Material current cash payout	_____	_____
Longer-term performance if shorter-term focus will restrict return	_____	_____
Liquidity—assurance that you can obtain current cash for this asset if necessary	_____	_____

Tax preference   _____ _____

Your independence from hands-on management   _____ _____

Finally, rate from 0 to 100 your ability to hold investments for longer-term results in the face of prevailing highly negative market sentiment   _____ _____

Personal Property

Enter dollar amount or value:

	Client I	Client II	Joint
Home furnishings	_____	_____	_____
Automobiles	_____	_____	_____
Jewelry	_____	_____	_____
Coins & stamps	_____	_____	_____
Clothing, furs	_____	_____	_____
Antiques	_____	_____	_____
Boat, airplane	_____	_____	_____
Other:			
_____	_____	_____	_____
_____	_____	_____	_____
_____	_____	_____	_____
_____	_____	_____	_____
_____	_____	_____	_____

Real Estate

(Other than Ltd. Partnerships, REIT's, etc.)

	Residence	Property 1	Property 2	Property 3
Description	_____	_____	_____	_____
	_____	_____	_____	_____
Purchase price	_____	_____	_____	_____

Mortgage	Amt	_____	_____	_____	_____
	%	_____	_____	_____	_____
	Yrs	_____	_____	_____	_____
	Year taken	_____	_____	_____	_____
2nd mortgage	Amt	_____	_____	_____	_____
	%	_____	_____	_____	_____
	Yrs	_____	_____	_____	_____
	Year taken	_____	_____	_____	_____
Cost of improvements		_____	_____	_____	_____
Monthly income		_____	_____	_____	_____
Depreciation/month		_____	_____	_____	_____
Other exp./month		_____	_____	_____	_____
Prop. tax/year		_____	_____	_____	_____
Current market value		_____	_____	_____	_____
Owner (Client I, Client II, Joint)		_____	_____	_____	_____
When purchased		_____	_____	_____	_____
Received from estate?		_____	_____	_____	_____
Value at transfer		_____	_____	_____	_____
What are your plans for this property?		_____	_____	_____	_____

Cash and Cash Equivalents

Type	Owner	Institution	Maturity	Yield	Balance
_____		_____	_____	_____	_____
_____		_____	_____	_____	_____
_____		_____	_____	_____	_____
_____		_____	_____	_____	_____
_____		_____	_____	_____	_____
_____		_____	_____	_____	_____

Stocks and Stock Mutual Funds

List all purchases separately. If you have cost basis figures for your investments, please provide them at this time.

If you have inherited stock, list the date and valuation basis.

If your statements cover this information, please submit them to us. If the item is in a retirement account, please note this.

Stock	Owner	Shares Held	Purchase Date	Price/ Share	Shares Purchased	Current Price	Annual Dividend

For tax considerations, please list below any securities that were purchased at less than 50 percent of the stock's current market value:

Stock	Owner	Shares Held	Purchase Date	Price/ Share	Shares Purchased	Current Price

Bonds and Bond Mutual Funds

List all items separately. If your statements cover this information, please submit them to us. If the item is in a retirement account, please note this.

Bond	Owner	Face Value	Coupon Rate	Maturity Date	Purchase Date	Purchase Price

Capital Gains and Losses

List your capital gains and losses realized this year, as well as carryovers from prior years: (Please leave blank if you have furnished copies of your tax returns)

Long-Term Gain/Loss	Gain	Loss
Carryover:		

Short-Term Gain/Loss	Gain	Loss
_____	_____	_____
_____	_____	_____
_____	_____	_____
Carryover:	_____	_____

Children's Education Savings

Child	Type	Institution	Balance	Yield
_____	____	_____	_____	_____
_____	____	_____	_____	_____
_____	____	_____	_____	_____
_____	____	_____	_____	_____
_____	____	_____	_____	_____
_____	____	_____	_____	_____
_____	____	_____	_____	_____
_____	____	_____	_____	_____

Retirement Savings and Pension Plans

Qualified Accounts

Type of Plan	Owner	Contrib. Made by Employer	Contribution Made by You	Current Value	How Funded	Beneficiary
Money purchase	____	_____	_____	_____	_____	_____
Profit sharing	____	_____	_____	_____	_____	_____
401(k)	____	_____	_____	_____	_____	_____
Other	____	_____	_____	_____	_____	_____
IRA	____	_____	_____	_____	_____	_____
IRA	____	_____	_____	_____	_____	_____
IRA	____	_____	_____	_____	_____	_____

IRA _____ _____ _____ _____ _____ _____

IRA _____ _____ _____ _____ _____ _____

Nonqualified Savings

_____ _____ _____ _____ _____

_____ _____ _____ _____ _____

Pension Annuities

Type/Institution	Owner	Estimated Monthly Payment	Survivor Benefit?	Age of 1st Payment	Lump Sum Value (if available)
_____	_____	_____	_____	_____	_____
_____	_____	_____	_____	_____	_____
_____	_____	_____	_____	_____	_____

Notes and Mortgages Owed to You and Miscellaneous Investments

Owner	Date Loaned	Amount Loaned	Due Date	Balance Due	Interest Rate	Received Monthly
_____	_____	_____	_____	_____	_____	_____
_____	_____	_____	_____	_____	_____	_____
_____	_____	_____	_____	_____	_____	_____
_____	_____	_____	_____	_____	_____	_____
_____	_____	_____	_____	_____	_____	_____
_____	_____	_____	_____	_____	_____	_____
_____	_____	_____	_____	_____	_____	_____
_____	_____	_____	_____	_____	_____	_____

Other Investments

Owner	Date Purchased	Gross Equity	Debt Outstanding	Approximate Yield	Income Received Monthly
_____	_____	_____	_____	_____	_____
_____	_____	_____	_____	_____	_____
_____	_____	_____	_____	_____	_____
_____	_____	_____	_____	_____	_____
_____	_____	_____	_____	_____	_____
_____	_____	_____	_____	_____	_____

Liabilities Owed by You Other Than Mortgages

Owed to	Owed by	Amount Borrowed	Due Date	Balance Due	Interest Rate	Monthly Payment
_____	_____	_____	_____	_____	_____	_____
_____	_____	_____	_____	_____	_____	_____
_____	_____	_____	_____	_____	_____	_____
_____	_____	_____	_____	_____	_____	_____
_____	_____	_____	_____	_____	_____	_____
_____	_____	_____	_____	_____	_____	_____
_____	_____	_____	_____	_____	_____	_____
_____	_____	_____	_____	_____	_____	_____

Business Interest or Professional Practice

Name and address of business or practice _____

_____

Sole proprietorship_____   Partnership_____   Sub S_____   Corporation_____

What would happen to your business in the event of a long disability or your death? Would you want it retained by your heirs, sold, or dissolved?

_____

_____

_____

_____

What is your share of the present market value of the business? _____

Do you expect your share of the business to change (i.e., bringing in partners, losing partners, etc.)?

_____

What are the growth prospects for your business?

Short term   _____

Longer term   _____

What amount would your estate receive if you were to die (liquidation value)?

_____

Do you have a buy/sell or stock redemption agreement? _____

What is the purchase price? _____

Is there an escalation clause to provide for increasing values? _____

Is the agreement funded? _____

With what vehicle? _____

How much? _____

Do you have a profit sharing plan or other retirement savings plan within your business? _____

If not, have you considered implementing one? _____

How many employees (including yourself) would be eligible _____ are vested _____ in the plan?

Is there any other information relating to your business that you feel is relevant (are there potential liabilities, lawsuits, assets you plan to buy or sell, etc.)?

_____

_____

_____

_____

_____

_____

Life Insurance

Please enter the following information as best you can. If possible, provide copies of your policies. In the column for "type" below, enter whole life, term, universal, etc. Also note that the information for each policy, numbered 1 through 8 continues below the first section.

	Insured	Paid by Self or Employer	Company	Face Amount	Type	Cash Value	Annual Prem.
1.							
2.							
3.							
4.							
5.							
6.							
7.							
8.							

	Beneficiary	Client I's Coverage	Client II's Coverage	Annual Dividends	Amount Borrowed	Borrowing Rate
1.						
2.						
3.						
4.						
5.						
6.						
7.						
8.						

Disability Insurance

Insured	Company	Monthly Benefit	Annual Premium	Waiting Period

Health Insurance, HMOs, and Other Healthcare

Insured	Company	Provided by Self or Empl.	Type of Coverage	Insurability Renewable?	Until What Age?	Annual Premium
_____	_____	_____	_____	_____	_____	_____
_____	_____	_____	_____	_____	_____	_____
_____	_____	_____	_____	_____	_____	_____
_____	_____	_____	_____	_____	_____	_____
_____	_____	_____	_____	_____	_____	_____
_____	_____	_____	_____	_____	_____	_____

Property and Casualty Insurance

Type	Company	Coverage	Annual Premium	Date Last Updated
Homeowners	_____	_____	_____	_____
Auto #1	_____	_____	_____	_____
Auto #2	_____	_____	_____	_____
Auto #3	_____	_____	_____	_____
Excess liability	_____	_____	_____	_____
Other: _____	_____	_____	_____	_____

Please describe insurance you may have through your business (funding buy/sell agreement, servicing your share of debt, etc.) or other insurance you own or have considered purchasing.

_____

_____

_____

Are there any unusual risks that you feel threaten your financial security? Explain:

_____

Income

Please estimate for the current tax year (12 months).

		Client I	Client II	Other
Employment:	Salary	_____	_____	_____
	Commissions	_____	_____	_____
	Bonus	_____	_____	_____
Interest & dividend income		_____	_____	_____
Private pension benefits		_____	_____	_____
Social Security		_____	_____	_____
Deferred compensation		_____	_____	_____
Business interests (net income)		_____	_____	_____
Real estate (net income)		_____	_____	_____
Trusts		_____	_____	_____
Alimony/child support		_____	_____	_____
Life insurance proceeds		_____	_____	_____
Other: _____		_____	_____	_____
_____		_____	_____	_____
_____		_____	_____	_____
_____		_____	_____	_____
_____		_____	_____	_____

By what percentage do you estimate your income will grow? Do you reasonably expect your income in any of these areas to change beyond cost-of-living adjustments in either the short term or the long term (up until retirement)? Explain:

_____

_____

_____

Do you have any benefits or perks (other than insurance and retirement funding covered above) that are business-related (i.e., company car or house, inexpensive loans, etc.)? Do you have any other sources of income that are not listed above (regular and substantial gifts, etc.)? Explain:

_____

_____

_____

Expenses

Please estimate the following expenses. Enter amounts either for year or for month. If your business pays for any of the expenses, please note the amount it pays (e.g., car expenses).

	Per Year	*Per Month*
Housing		
Rent	_____	_____
Mortgage	_____	_____
Property taxes	_____	_____
Repairs & purchases	_____	_____
Utilities	_____	_____
Condo fee	_____	_____
Furnishings	_____	_____
Other (gardener, domestic, etc.)	_____	_____
Clothing	_____	_____
Food	_____	_____
Transportation		
Gas	_____	_____
Repairs	_____	_____
Commuting	_____	_____
Other	_____	_____
Parental support	_____	_____

Insurance

    Medical & dental   _____   _____

    Disability   _____   _____

    Life   _____   _____

    Property/casualty   _____   _____

    Other   _____   _____

Medical & dental expenses   _____   _____

In-town recreation & entertainment   _____   _____

Vacations   _____   _____

Gifts   _____   _____

Charitable contributions   _____   _____

Adult education   _____   _____

Day-to-day personal expenses

    Please estimate the amount of cash you draw from checking or credit cards for everyday needs not previously covered   _____   _____

Professional fees   _____   _____

Children

    Child care   _____   _____

    Education   _____   _____

    Other (camps, lessons, etc.)   _____   _____

Loan payments (nonmortgage)   _____   _____

Hobby expenses   _____   _____

Retirement contributions   _____   _____

Other: _____   _____   _____

    _____   _____   _____

    _____   _____   _____

Savings and Investments

(Estimate the amounts you saved over the year, exclusive of pension contributions.)

Are there any reasons to believe that any of your current ongoing living expenses will change drastically (other than for inflation effects) in either the short term or long term (due to a move, etc.)? Explain:

_____

_____

_____

Do you have any larger expenses on the horizon (home improvement, major purchases, large repayment of a debt, etc.)? Explain and give projected outlays:

_____

_____

_____

Are any of the costs listed above business-related? Should any be considered apart from your personal life? Explain:

_____

_____

_____

Estate Information

Do you have a will? ____   Date drawn ____   Date last reviewed ____

Does your spouse have a will? ____   Date drawn ____   Date last reviewed ____

Are you a citizen of the United States? ____

Is your spouse a citizen of the United States? ____

Do you expect any inheritances? ____   Source _____

    How much is expected? _____

Does your spouse expect any inheritances?   Source _____

    How much is expected? _____

Do you want to make any gifts or pass an estate to your heirs? Are your plans expressed in your will? Explain:

_____

_____

_____

Trust Information

Have you created any trusts? ____

If so, please explain below, including the type, amount, date created, and beneficiary:

_____

_____

_____

_____

Are you the beneficiary of any trusts? ____

If so, please explain below, including the type, donor, amount, and annual income:

_____

_____

_____

_____

Congratulations, you have finished providing the information we will use in developing your plan. Wait several days before returning the questionnaire to us. This will give you time to reflect on your answers or jot down other ideas or questions that may crop up.

Index